HOME COLOR HARMONY

BETTERWAY BOOKS
Cincinnati, Ohio

Front cover photographs:
(top left and bottom) Eaglemoss Publications/Tif Hunter,
(top right) Eaglemoss Publications/Graham Rae.
Back cover: (left) Dulux, (top right) Insight, London Picture Library/Michelle Garrett,
(bottom right) Ariadne, Holland.

Photographs page 1 Elizabeth Whiting and Associates/Michael Dunne,
2 Eaglemoss/Graham Rae, 3 Eaglemoss/Steve Tanner, 4 René Stoeltie.

First published in North America
in 1998 by Betterway Books
an imprint of F&W Publications, Inc.
1507 Dana Avenue
Cincinnati, Ohio 45207
1-800-289-0963

ISBN 1-55870-499-X

Printed in Hong Kong

10 9 8 7 6 5 4 3 2 1

CONTENTS

A QUICK LOOK AT COLOR BASICS

Recognizing colors 5
Understanding color 11
Choosing a color scheme 17

WORK WITHIN A COLOR GROUP

Provençal colors 23
Sunrise and sunset colors 29
Sea and sky colors 35
Pastel colors 41
Earth colors 45
Natural neutrals 51
Berry colors 57
Dried flower colors 63

MIX AND MATCH INDIVIDUAL HUES

Riotous red 69
In the pink 75
Terracotta 81
Peach and apricot 87
Yellow 91
Going green 97
Tempting turquoise 103
The blues 109
Sparkling white 115
Naturally brown 121

INDEX

INDEX 127

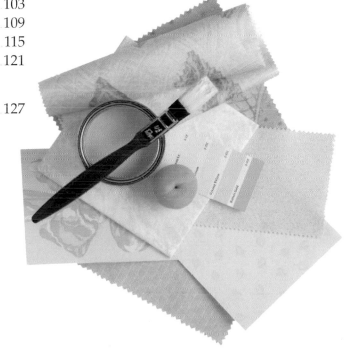

RECOGNIZING COLOURS

Colour is an important and personal part of our everyday lives, but its effects are often underestimated and its potential neglected. Colour influences the way that we feel – bold, bright colours are stimulating; pale, cool colours are soothing. Bright primary reds, yellows and blues, fine for a child's playroom, would be inappropriate in a bedroom where pastels or muted colours would be more restful.

Colours like red, pink and orange seem warm, while blues and greys produce a cooler effect. The 'warmness' and 'coolness' of colours can be dramatic: in a controlled experiment, people living in a blue room set the heating thermostat four degrees higher than the people in a red room.

Colour also affects the way we see things – warm colours such as reds and oranges bring surfaces forward, so could be used to make a large room seem smaller and cosier. Cool colours, such as blues and blue-greens, are recessive – a small room will look larger if you choose cool colours.

The personality of colour

The effects of colour on our perception can be quite dramatic. If two boxes are painted red and green, people will judge the red one to be heavier than the green. The colours you choose reflect your personality – extroverts tend to feel happier in rooms containing strong bright colours because they need stimulating environments. Introverts are generally more at home with subdued, earthy colours.

Colour is further complicated by lighting. The white interiors and exteriors that look fresh and bright in brilliant Mediterranean-type weather look dull and dingy under winter skies.

▼ **Bright, happy colours**
Sunny yellow walls and a profusion of patterns in vivid contrasting colours give this living room a happy, comfortable atmosphere.

The language of colour

This section introduces the language of colour. First the main colour groups used by interior designers are described. Some of these groups overlap: for example, earth colours are generally warm, but many of them could also be described as muted.

▶ Provençal colours

The most important colours for the artist are the primaries - red, yellow and blue - which are most clearly evident in Provençal prints. In their pure forms they are the most brilliant colours and can be used together to create a bright, singing effect. Small touches can be used to give zest to an otherwise subdued scheme. A touch of stop sign red will brighten up earth colours; a splash of yellow will set off a pastel blue scheme.

▲ Sunrise and sunset

Reds, pinks, oranges and yellows are the warm colours. They remind us of sunshine and firelight, and create a cosy, welcoming atmosphere. Warm colours 'advance', that is they seem nearer than cool colours. Use them to make a large room seem smaller and friendlier or to brighten a north-facing room. The closer a warm colour is to the primary colours of red or yellow, the stronger it will be. For the country look the softer peaches, pinks and primrose yellow are the most appropriate.

▲ Sea and sky
These are the cool colours – the blues, blue-greens and greens that are opposite the warm colours on the colour wheel. Evoking blue skies, clear water and winter forests, they are the colours to use if you want to create a cool, calm atmosphere. Cool colours recede – they seem further away than warm colours so should be used if you want a room to seem larger and more spacious than it is. Bright, well lit rooms can take cool colours without appearing cold, but be careful in north-facing rooms or rooms that don't have much light, as cool colours can look rather bleak.

◄ Pastel colours
These are tints of pure colours – pure colours lightened with a lot of white. Red lightened with white becomes pink, green lightened with white becomes apple green, orange becomes apricot, yellow becomes primrose. They are soft, gentle colours reminiscent of ice-cream or sugared almonds. All the pastels harmonize with one another because they have the same tonal value. They also blend well with muted colours.

▶ **Earth colours**
Earth pigments were originally made from natural clays and their names survive – burnt sienna, ochre and umber. Earth colours are the colours of autumn – muted russets, the red of dried rose petals, drab greens and browns. They particularly lend themselves to decorating schemes with a rugged country appeal.

▼ **Neutral colours**
Used on their own, or as partners with another colour scheme, neutrals blend together well and create an unobtrusive background for furniture, pictures and flowers. Look for pebble colours, beige, grey, buff, off-white, slate grey and sepia. A good off-white is a particularly useful colour.

◀ Berry colours
These are rich, jewel-like
colours – deep purples,
velvety greens, reds and
plums and golds – the
colours of oriental carpets.
Often seen in the public
areas of splendid historic
residences, these colours
can add a richness and
depth to smaller, modern
homes. Luxuriously
textured fabrics like velvet
and satin look wonderful
in these shades. Use rich
velvet to cover a small
footstool or armchair, or
curtains in stripes of these
opulent colours to create a
dramatic effect in a low-
key room.

▲ Dried flower colours
When black or grey are
added to primary colours,
the result is a muted
colour or shade. Pastels
and flower colours are
popular with interior
designers, but the softer
versions of these colours –
the colours of dried
flowers, for example – are
much easier to work with.
These old, slightly faded
colours harmonize with
one another, and you can
use a lot of them together.

GLOSSARY OF TERMS

Accent colour This adds a touch of colour that is different from the predominant scheme. Any bright colour will provide an accent to a neutral scheme: a warm red accent adds zest to a predominantly cool green room.

Broken colour This is colour applied in such a way that the underlying colour shows through. With paint you can achieve this effect by dragging, ragging and sponging. At a distance the eye blends the shades to create a single colour.

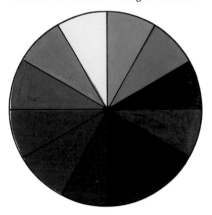

▲ ▼ **Neutrals and muted shades** *The cream walls and brown wood provide a perfect background for flowers and kitchenware.*

Colour wheel The conventional way of showing how primary and secondary colours relate to each other and how they combine to make other colours. It is a useful aid to understanding how best to combine and mix colours.

Complementary or contrast colours These appear opposite each other on the colour wheel and have a special relationship. If mixed together in equal quantities they compete. Placed side by side they enhance each other, so that green and red, for instance, look greener and redder respectively.

Cool colours These are the colours to use if you want a room to have a cool, calm atmosphere – they are the greens, blue-greens and blues of forests, water and skies. Cool colours always appear further away than warm ones making a small room seem spacious. They look best in rooms with lots of natural light; in dark rooms cool colours seem cold.

Harmonious colours Any two, three or four colours lying next to each other on the colour wheel combine easily. One harmonious group is pink, apricot, peach and gold, which work together as there is a common theme between the colours.

Muted colours Adding black or grey to the pure colours of the wheel produces subtle or muted colours like mustard yellow, russet, sage green, plum and blackberry. Because of their black content, they look particularly good accented with black.

Neutral colours Neutrals range from white through creams, beiges, tans and browns, and from the palest silver grey through to black. They make perfect backgrounds for positive colours, or you can create attractive all-neutral schemes.

Pastel colours Pastels are the pretty, chalky colours produced by adding lots of white to other colours: thus pink comes from red, lilac from purple and apricot from orange. You can successfully combine lots of pastels in one decorative theme as they all contain quantities of white.

Primary colours The 'painter's primaries' are red, yellow and blue. All the other colours can be produced by combinations of these, plus white and black.

Secondary colours These are produced by mixing equal amounts of adjacent primaries: blue and yellow gives green; yellow and red gives orange; red and blue gives purple.

Shade This is produced when black is added to a colour. For example, muted colours are shades of primaries and secondaries.

Tint Adding any colour to white produces a tint, though the term is used loosely to describe a shade.

Tone A tone is a lighter or darker version of a colour (a tint or a shade). Colours with the same tonal value have a harmonious relationship – they contain the same amounts of white or black.

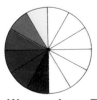

Warm colours The reds, pinks, oranges and yellows associated with sunshine and firelight. Use them to brighten a sunless room or to make a large room cosier.

UNDERSTANDING COLOUR

Some people are blessed with a natural feeling for colour. They instinctively know which colours will go together, how to balance tones and when to introduce a contrasting accent shade. They effortlessly mix and match colours to create a comfy bedroom or a stylish living room. For the rest of us, it is more often than not a case of trial and error. But it needn't be, if you take a little time to understand a few simple rules. With the help of a colour wheel, you can analyse colour relationships and learn why a particular arrangement of colours works. This will help you to use colour with confidence and to plan or rectify a colour scheme when your intuition lets you down.

▼ *Contrasts and harmonies*
A rich palette of colours is assembled in this arrangement of full-blown roses. The yellow, orange, apricot and pink coloured blooms relate harmoniously because they come from the same sector of the colour wheel. The sharp green, which comes from the opposite side of the wheel, provides a contrast.

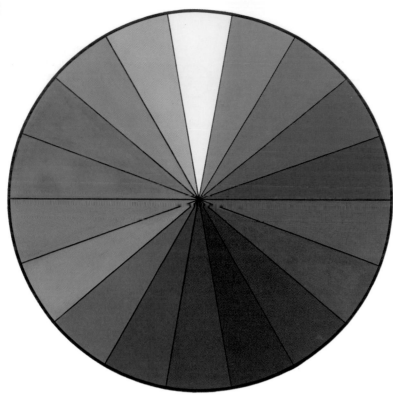

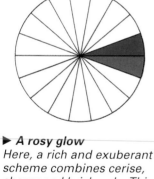

The colour wheel

The colour wheel is a traditional diagrammatic illustration of colour relationships, and a useful aid to decorating your home. The three primary colours are red, yellow and blue. Colours which fall between two primaries have a harmonious relationship, while those that occur opposite one another on the wheel are complementary. Colours on either side of a primary become less harmonious the further apart they are.

▶ A rosy glow

Here, a rich and exuberant scheme combines cerise, cherry and brick reds. This is not an obvious combination of colours, but they work well together because of their harmonious relationship. You will find them all located between red and orange on the colour wheel. If you look closely at the picture you will find that the colours have a similar tonal value, so that none overwhelms the others. In fact, the only tonal contrast is provided by the dark wooden bedstead.

▲ Sea and sky

The slightly muted shades of blue and blue-green are a particularly soothing range of colours. They are very compatible and can be used boldly and freely in creating a traditional country setting. In this cottage kitchen, the sky blue predominates on the walls and ceiling, acting as the perfect foil for the blue-green paintwork on the door and window.

Small touches of a strong reddish purple act as a sparky accent colour in the overall scheme, on the wall by the door, on the tartan curtain under the sink and in the heather on the table.

Harmonious colours

Most people find colour schemes based on a limited range of colours pleasing and comfortable to live with. Fortunately, these harmonious colour schemes are also the easiest to put into practice without taking too many design risks.

Monochrome schemes

The simplest kind of harmony relies on arrangements based on a single colour. These are virtually foolproof colour schemes which share many of the qualities of a neutral scheme, in that they are restful, because the colours blend well, and work in almost any location or style of house.

If you want to develop a one-colour scheme, start from the colour of the existing upholstery or an ornament, or even a new textile that appeals to you. Even within a single colour, you can find a rich variety of subtly different colours called shades, which range from cool to warm, through muted to intense. The paler and darker versions of the same shade are known as tones.

You could, for example, choose a pale shade for the walls and ceiling which will reflect the light. You can then add interest and emphasis by using darker or lighter tones of the same colour to pick out architectural details like skirting boards and door frames. Still richer or more intense shades of the same colour can be used to draw attention to a particularly attractive feature such as an intricate moulding.

Related harmonies

The second kind of harmonious scheme is made up from groups of colours that lie between the primary colours on the colour wheel. Look, for example, at the colours between blue and yellow and you will find a range of blue-greens and green-blues. The eye runs very easily between them without an abrupt transition. Even when they are taken out of sequence, a group of these related colours always goes well together.

The scope of this scheme can be considerably extended by introducing shades of these colours in lighter and darker tones and more muted mixtures. Once again, you need to work in gentle steps between tones, to eliminate visual jolts. Save extreme contrasts for small touches of emphasis. A very light or very dark tone of one of the colours you are using can become an accent to give a lift to an otherwise restrained scheme.

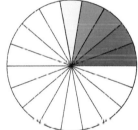

▶ Sunflower bright
In this sunny, summery corner, terracotta and sunflower yellow checks sit happily together on a cushion and throw. By working with a restricted palette of colours, it has been possible to create a very well coordinated arrangement which still has plenty of vitality.

If you study the picture, you will find that the main colours are present in different tones on various items; pale terracotta and daffodil yellow feature in the cushion, while deeper tones of the same shades are woven in the throw. As the odd colour, turquoise sizzles against a red from the other side of the colour wheel.

Complementary colours

Many people want more excitement from their surroundings than the essentially soothing and restrained settings created by monochrome schemes or those based on adjacent, harmonious colours. You may favour calmness in some rooms, like the bedrooms or hallway, but seek a more energetic look in the living room, play room or kitchen.

The complementary pairs – the colours opposite each other on the colour wheel – provide an effective way of creating a satisfying colour scheme which has a bit more zest. Their special relationship means that when they are used together they bring out the best in each other. So red used with green has more punch than it has on its own.

Schemes for the adventurous

Complementary pairings from opposite sides of the colour wheel are inspiring if you want to introduce visual drama into your surroundings. For a vivid scheme, look to the brightest shades, like the colours shown on our colour wheel. These high contrast schemes can be tricky and need to be handled with care. Use the colours in different tones, and introduce neutrals such as grey, white, beige or brown to take some of the harsh edge off the arrangement.

Muted complementaries

Some of the most enjoyable colour schemes can be devised around the less strident complementary pairs. These muted shades are nearer to those seen in nature, earth colours like brown and terracotta and dried flower colours like lilac, pale blue, peach and primrose.

Terracotta finds its complementary partner in a bright blue. Yellow ochre looks good with a pale blue. Khaki green is set off by iris purple. The possibilities of such pairings are almost infinite. Using them, you can create colourful schemes which are easy to live with, but never boring.

Complementaries as accents

Accent colours are introduced in small quantities to add spice to a scheme. The complementary of the main colour is a particularly effective accent. A splash of red in a largely green scheme will result in both colours being experienced more intensely. The red will look redder, the green greener.

The warm colours, which are more advancing than the cool shades, have considerable impact even in small quantities. So very small amounts of red will liven up a green room, while larger amounts of green will be required to have the same impact in a red room.

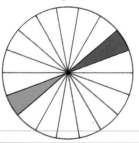

▼ **Terracotta and sky blue** Terracotta and orange find their complementary partners in the blue range. These colours have a wonderful resonance and bring out the best in each other – the terracotta looks richer and the sky blue brighter. They can be used as accent colours to each other, or as the basis of a colour scheme, in a kitchen, for example, where blue paint is paired with quarry tiles.

◄ **Violet and green** *Violet and the cool reds are precisely complemented by various shades of bright green. Here, the sparkling colours of the books and stationery on the desk, and the more sombre, muted tones in the floral wallpaper and fireplace, exploit these relationships very successfully. It illustrates beautifully how toning complementary partnerships hold good regardless of the strength of the colours.*

▼ **Yellow and purple**
This is a particularly lively pairing of complementary colours that can be used to produce some very rich and exciting effects in decorating. In these wacky fabrics, it is interesting to see how well a whole range of vibrant colours work together to produce a joyful outcome. The grey cats introduce a vital neutral note.

Problem-solving with colour

A knowledge of colour relationships will help you to solve interior design problems. Take a common dilemma. A room is newly redecorated but it still doesn't feel quite right. You have chosen harmonious colours from the same sector of the colour wheel, so they should go together. It may be that there are too many contrasts of tone and shade, so the eye is constantly jolted as it moves from one area to another.

To remedy this, you can ensure a gentler gradation from one colour to the next, and restore a harmonious balance to the room, by introducing a few intermediate shades and tones into the scheme on cushions, shades and rugs.

▼ ▶ Seeing red – or green and red
Sometimes, a colour scheme is disappointing because it plays too safe and ends up looking rather dull. In which case, a harmonious tonal contrast can be deliberately introduced as light relief. That is exactly what has happened in this vividly pink room. Although it could never be tame, the shock of other reds brings it to life.

Another solution is to inject the appropriate complementary colour from the opposite side of the colour wheel – in this case green – to add the necessary verve to the scheme. Here, the green in the floral fabric works with the red in the tablecloth to give the setting a lift.

CHOOSING A COLOUR SCHEME

Colour is the most important element in any decorative scheme, yet it is an area that most of us shy away from. It is the most exciting, the most flexible and the least expensive aspect of home design and yet we so often opt for neutral colours with the occasional splash of colour or pattern. Colour sets the mood and style of a room, and gives it personality. It affects the impact the room has on people, the way they feel in it and the way they behave. And the colours you use will reflect your personality.

▼ **Helping plan a colour scheme**
There are many aids to help you select the right colours. Paint manufacturers produce colour charts, and shops will let you have samples of papers and fabrics. Magazines and catalogues are another invaluable source of inspiration.

Practical colour choices

Colour also has practical functions: the choice of colour can make a room seem larger or smaller, cooler or warmer. Colour also has strong associations in our minds. For example, pink is seen as a clean colour and is often used in bathrooms, while red, brown and green, which are associated with food, are favourite colours in kitchens.

Many of our reactions to colour are derived from associations with the natural world – greens and blues are seen as cool and soothing, while reds and yellows are seen as warm and energetic.

Starting from scratch

Most of us have dreamt of having the opportunity to design and decorate a room from scratch, having an absolutely free hand. But, surprisingly, this is the most difficult task of all – it can be like the painter who is faced with a blank canvas. Fortunately, in real life, decisions are usually made within an existing scheme.

If you are considering a new decorative scheme the first thing to do is to look long and hard at the room you are going to decorate, listing its good and bad points, and thinking about things like lighting and how the room will be used. To help you do this, answer the questions in the checklist overleaf and start from there.

Ways to choose colour

There are a number of tactics you can adopt to choose your colour scheme.

Personal preference We all have favourite colours. If yours is yellow, for example, and the room is very light, the colour may be too much for the room. Think about using yellow in a patterned fabric for the curtains or for soft furnishings instead of the walls.

Catalogues The major soft furnishing companies and paint and wallpaper manufacturers coordinate their colours and patterns, often with a style in mind. Looking at their catalogues, you may see a colour scheme that you like. Try to reproduce it using their products or something close to them.

Start with the accessories If you have some favourite accessories such as dried flowers or china, use their colours to help you pick a coordinating colour scheme. A treasured ornament or vase could be another starting point, or perhaps a patterned sofa or rug. In the bedroom, use bed linen as a basis for the scheme.

Three points to remember

Light affects the way you perceive colours. For example, a green which looks muted and has a blue tinge under strip lighting in the showroom may look warmer and more yellow in a sunny, south-facing room. A deep, holly-leaf green will look even darker and richer in a dark room, but will lose much of its intensity in a brightly-lit room. This is why it is so important to try out a large sample of the colour in the room in which you intend to use it.

Colours are affected and modified by surrounding colours, so while a bright blue may kill a subtle pink, a paler blue will look wonderful. This is because mixtures of colours of equal tone look good together – pastel pinks, yellows and peaches, for example.

If, when you have bought the paint, the particular colour looks too bright, you can create a balance by adding small amounts of white or black paint, mixing well and testing. This takes courage but the results can be rewarding.

Combinations of strong, bright reds, yellows and blues also look harmonious and well balanced. This is because they have the same depth of colour and brightness.

The amount of colour affects the way you see it. While it might be difficult to live with four walls of bright orange or strong pink, splashes of these colours add zest to an all-white or single-colour scheme.

COLOUR SCHEME CHECKLIST

There are some general dos and don'ts that you should consider before you decide on your new colour scheme.

Is it a frequently used area?	**YES**	Choose peaceful, easy colours on walls; patterned or neutral flooring.
	NO	A bold splash of colour is a nice change; elegant pastels or cream can be used where they won't get too dirty.
Does it face north?	**YES**	Warm it up with red, sunny yellow or peach.
	NO	Cool blues and greens will be balanced by the warm light.
Is the ceiling low?	**YES**	Paint it white or cream to give the room height; a vertically striped paper would help.
	NO	You could take the wall colour/paper right over the ceiling for a total look.
Is the room smaller than you would like?	**YES**	Keep to clear, pale tones, small or self patterns – go for texture to add interest.
	NO	Link different parts of the room by splashes of the same strong tone against bold contrasts.
Does it have enough light?	**YES**	You can choose dark colours and rich woods like mahogany.
	NO	Reflect the light with white/cream walls, pine or light wood and a mirror.
Is it a 'first impressions' area such as an entrance hall or lobby?	**YES**	Give a welcome glow with warm pinks, reds and happy yellow.
	NO	Indulge yourself – choose your favourite colour.
Is it crowded, with furniture, knick-knacks and people?	**YES**	Keep it simple. A one-colour scheme to act as a background to the chaos.
	NO	Add interest and life with bright splashes of colour and strong patterns
Do you or any of your family work in it?	**YES**	Be business-like. Plain uncluttered surroundings are less distracting.
	NO	Pretty soft pastels give a restful look; dress it up with florals.
Do children spend a lot of time in the room?	**YES**	Stimulate their senses with bright, interesting patterns and bold colours.
	NO	Get the opinions of the rest of the family before you do anything final.

A single-colour scheme

One of the simplest ways of working out a single-colour scheme is to start with one major item and use a limited palette of colours. Start collecting samples of paints, fabrics and carpets. Look for your chosen colour and related tones of other colours. Look for small, subtle patterns as these are easier to mix and match than stronger, brighter ones.

If you are too rigorous about finding related tones and colours, the result could be boring. Add interest with subtle textures, apply the paint with a broken colour paint effect on the walls, for example, or a berber weave carpet.

Splashes of a contrasting colour lift a scheme. In a blue room, for example, orange cushions or a woven rug with orange shades will add a touch of warmth and excitement to the scheme. (Orange is on the warm side of the spectrum – a little will have a lot of impact.) All these separate elements come together to create a satisfying whole – even flowers can be part of the scheme.

▼ **Fresh green scheme**
A The freshness and greenness is picked up in the key component – the delightful green gingham covers on the simple, stylish high-backed dining chairs. The roman blinds are made in crisp white linen.
B Emulsion/latex paint on the walls and ceiling is a good choice. The walls are pale apple green and the ceiling is white with a hint of green which picks up the predominant colour and creates an illusion of height.
C The other elements maintain the single-colour theme – framed prints are of verdant spring and summer foliage, the glass table has metal legs with a bluey-green patina and a brass urn has a turquoise surface.
D The warm, honeyed tones of the parquet floor act as a counterweight to the prevailing cool tones. Buff paint is used to pick out the panelling on the corner cupboard.

Starting from a pattern

By using a multi-coloured pattern as your jumping-off point you can create a more ambitious colour scheme using the expertise and colour sense of the designer.

The people who design fabrics and wallpapers are experts at handling colour, they know what goes with what, and which proportions work best, so by pulling out colours from a pattern and using them in the same proportions you can create a harmonious scheme.

Manufacturers supply ranges of co-ordinating fabrics – large prints with small prints and plains and stripes – which provide ready-made solutions to mix-and-match requirements.

Floral patterns

The key to this room with its warm, rosy and russet colours, is the comfortable armchair, covered in a large floral pattern. The main colours on the pattern have been used as a starting point to build the colour scheme. Here the large golden-headed flowers are the dominant element. This is matched by the golden tones of the polished pine floorboards – the single largest area of solid colour in the room.

On the walls a smaller sprigged pattern in the same colourways echoes the larger print with a still smaller floral wallpaper border hung at picture rail level. The rich coral on the walls of the hallway and above the picture rail adds warmth and drama to an otherwise simple scheme.

Coral is used for the curtains which are self-patterned, adding subtle texture. This coral note has been drawn from a minor theme in the main fabric, but contributes a main theme to the room decor. Remember that colours used near a window have a more powerful influence as the colour tints the light which permeates the whole room. Here the coral curtains give the room a warm glow.

Using the colours matched by the fabric designer gives you the confidence to put together unusual colours.

▼ **Coordinated fabric and papers**
Although the patterns are different the colours all blend in this range.

▲ Pattern used as the starting point

A strongly patterned fabric is the key to this colour scheme.

A The warm ochre and coral of the floral print on the armchair are the basis for the rest of the colours used in this scheme.

B The pinky-red of the carnations is picked up in the rich coral walls and damask curtains. The upholstery fabric has been used for the tie-back.

C The floors are warm polished natural wood.

D A coordinating fabric, wallpaper and border in a smaller floral bouquet print keep within the colour scheme.

E Floral prints in antiqued golden frames pick up the theme colours.

What colours do you like?

For a lucky few, choosing colours is easy. They are born with a natural sense of colour, and can remember shades of a colour so precisely, they can match a pinky-red without a sample, while the rest of us would arrive home with a tomato red that was quite wrong. However, some of us don't even know what colours we like, because we have never really thought about it.

Faced with re-decorating a room, don't be overcome with panic and take the easy way out by going for what you had before. Spend time thinking about it and looking for ideas – you may discover that you have strong colour preferences.

Start by looking in your wardrobe – your clothes probably fall into a few distinctive colour groups. Another trick is to leaf through magazines and catalogues marking the pages which show room schemes that you like. A few days later, look through the pages you have marked – you will find that these too fall into definite colour categories.

Looking for inspiration

There are many ways of finding a hook for a colour scheme. Look at the objects you gather around you. For example, have you got a collection of pots and jugs, or do you have paintings or prints on your walls. All these things can be used as the basis of a colour scheme – they also reveal your colour preferences.

If you still aren't sure, experiment by introducing small touches of colour – this is particularly effective in plain rooms. Look around for objects in the colours you are contemplating using – pots, paintings or even flowers. Arrange them in the room and live with them for a while to see how you feel about living with the colour permanently.

▲ Blue and white details
You don't need to spend a great deal of money to bring colour into your home. A plain white bathroom is transformed by adding pale blue baskets, pots and a soap holder. The blue hydrangeas are an inspired touch.

◀ Pastels and primaries
The spring colours of this room reflect the owner's taste which is revealed in the painting on the wall, and in the collection of glass vases and plates on the shelf beneath.

PROVENÇAL COLOURS

The hot, sun-drenched regions that border the Mediterranean in the south of France have given us a vibrant palette of deeply saturated colours: the primaries – red, yellow and blue, and an exciting range of associated colours including deep aquamarines, brilliant saffron yellow and rich, russety reds. These are the colours of nature, colours taken from the surrounding landscape; the 'impure', modified colours of earth pigments and natural organic dyes.

The warm colours

On the warm side of the palette there are wonderful reds, golds and yellows. The reds reflect the ferrous earths of the region, rust reds and the reds of ripe apples, warm brick reds, with here and there a splash of the scarlet of wayside poppies or the geraniums crowded into painted pots around doorways and tumbling out of window boxes. The yellows are warm and spicy, ranging from palest butter shades through the pale golds of wheat and baked clay, mustards and ochres to the dazzling yellow of ripe sunflowers.

Cool colours

The cool side of the palette is equally seductive – from the intense blue of a cloudless sky and the cool jade-green of deep tranquil seas to purples, lilacs and lavenders. The greens are the soft, silvery greens of olive leaves, and the variegated shades of orchards and vineyards that can be seen from every roadside.

Muted colours

In the height of summer, a light dust covers the countryside, and exposure to wind and sun weathers paintwork; these processes producing another range of muted shades – dusty pinks, flat olive greens, the azure of mist-shrouded hills, and the 'old' blue of wisteria.

▼ **Primary influence**
The vibrant colours of Provence, inspired by the countryside of the region, centre on the primaries – red, blue and yellow – and their associated shades and colours.

A painter's paradise

It was the rich palette of colours and the special brilliance of the light which attracted some of the greatest painters of the time to the region at the end of the last century. We see these colours in the paintings of Vincent van Gogh, who describes his response to the colours of the region in his letters. 'As for the blue,' he says, 'it goes from the deepest royal blue in the water to the blue of forget-me-nots, to cobalt, especially to a pale, transparent blue, to blue-green to blue-violet.' This then is the palette available to the home decorator seeking to introduce some of the magic of Provence into their home.

▲ As for the blue

The blue, so admired by Van Gogh, gives these walls a vibrancy which recalls the brilliant blue of the sea and sky on summer days. The rest of the room is decorated completely in white to allow the blue to dominate the room, but a dash of red or yellow would not go amiss.

▼ Merry Provence

In a rustic room, with unplastered walls painted white, vibrant Provençal colours create a bright and cheerful impression.

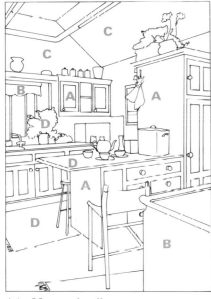

▲ ▶ Mustard yellow

A Warm, mustard yellow is typical of the region, creating a sunny effect which will warm up the coldest room.
B Red, the hottest of the primaries, should only be used in splashes, as here – a little red goes a long way, and needs to be balanced by a large area of white or cool blue.
C White is the perfect foil for warm red and yellow, lightening the effect and preventing the colours from overpowering the room.
D Flashes of green, blue and grey work with the white to temper the heat of the red and yellow.

▼ French flash
The tablecloth, with its lively flashes of colour, is a striking Provençal touch, the more subtle balance of cool and warm, green and yellow, is another of the images of Provence.

The authentic look

The people of Provence use these colours unselfconsciously. They are the colours of their countryside, the colours they were brought up with. It is a harmonious orchestration of colour, texture and pattern which has evolved over generations: warm colours setting off cool; natural materials and painted surfaces used together; plain contrasting with pattern and texture. Colour is evident everywhere. On shutters, doors and other exterior woodwork, you'll find peeling paintwork in an intense sky blue, lavender or a bleached olive-green.

The rough plaster walls of country houses are simply whitewashed or given a thin coat of mustard yellow or rich brick red. Across a field of pale golden stubble you'll see a barn, its walls russet red trimmed with white, the roof ribbed with the variegated pinks, reds and greys of weathered pantiles. Even in the towns, buildings are given a wash of colour. Outside a pavement café bright yellow plastic chairs catch the eye, a pleasing contrast to the gaily striped blue-and-white awnings above.

Why these colours work

Bright unmodified primary colours, especially the warm primaries, red and yellow, are difficult to use and, in large quantities, can be tiring to live with. Reds and yellows tend to advance visually, making a room seem warm and

▲ Tips from the French
Blue and yellow is a very French combination and a successful warm-cool/ mix, which looks especially good with the fresh touch of the white tablecloth and wicker chairs.

◄ Red and yellow
Yellow walls and red shelves make this alcove look warm and bright. The white shelf brackets add a refreshing touch and link in with the plaster-work on the ceiling.

► Cooler temper
This bold balance of colour and pattern works well because the designs have the same energy and vitality. The hot red and yellow are tempered by cooler green and blue.

cosy, but overwhelming other colours. They are so energetic and vital that they should be used carefully, usually in small quantities and tempered with cool or neutral colours.

Blue, the cool primary, is less dominant and therefore easier to handle; it is a receding, soothing colour, which can open out a space, but used extensively in its pure form can make a room seem chilly and harsh.

If you want to use primaries on large areas, such as walls, the trick is to use them in a modified form – in Provence the reds used over large surfaces are earth reds and dusty pinks. Choose soft creamy or ochry yellows and blues tinged with pink, grey or green in preference to the true primaries.

The people of Provence have the knack of combining warm colours with cool colours – a simple but effective device which calms the hot colours and gives life to the cools. Blues and greens take the sting out of reds and yellows, while splashes of hot colours add zest to expanses of blue, purple or green.

Using the primary colours
A successful colour scheme depends on achieving harmony by balancing one colour with another; a large area of a cool colour against a smaller area of a warm colour, for example, or equal amounts of a warm and cool against a background of white.

The warm–cool balance is a useful one and almost always works, especially

with the intense primary reds, yellows and blues. Blue and yellow is a particularly successful, and very French combination. For a cheerful French country kitchen, team these colours with rough plaster walls, stone floors and basic pine furniture.

White is a useful foil for these vibrant colours, freshening and lightening their effect – blue and white, for example, looks fresh and clean. This combination can be a bit cool for everyday living, but is ideal for a warm, south-facing bedroom or bathroom, especially if you choose fabrics and surfaces with a textural quality to lend surface interest. Opt for rough plaster walls, slub linens and loosely woven cottons which create a very French look.

▲ **Red and green**
Intense green – the green of shutters and doors in southern France – is rich and elegant in a country house setting. Just a splash of red in the cushion and curtains balances nicely with all the green.

▶ Sun-drenched walls
A mixture of vibrant colours against a background of plain, yellow walls is a very warm and cheerful combination which recalls the sun-drenched regions of southern France.

▼ In the balance
A Verdigris, the colour of weathered copper, brass or bronze, is a natural colour which recalls the houses of the region. Against the warm yellow of the walls, it produces a very French balance of cool against warm.
B A small amount of hot red enforces the warm side of the balance, while a strong, purply blue matches it on the cool side.

SUNRISE AND SUNSET COLOURS

Some rooms seem warm and inviting, even on a chilly day when the inside temperature is not particularly high; but other rooms are never cosy and cheerful no matter how high the heating. The solution to this apparent contradiction lies in the colour scheme. Human beings are particularly sensitive to the effect of colour and no sooner does the eye take in a particular colour than the subconscious gets to work, raking up a complicated network of associations some going back to early childhood – which can affect us both emotionally and physically.

If you want a room to to look warm and cheerful, it is sensible to choose colours that make you feel warm and cheerful. These are the hot colours – reds, yellows and oranges. From them come the warm colours – the colours we associate with sunrise and sunset ranging from the palest pinks and primroses, to deep shades of peach, rich russets and pinky, brick reds. The down-to-earth Victorians knew perfectly well what they were about when they papered their dining rooms in deep reds and oranges; they felt these colours created a sense of well-being and warmth, which in turn helped them to feel comfortable, and allowed them to enjoy their food.

There is also a gradation between warm and cool colours – the blues and greens: some warm colours are cooler than others, while some cool colours are at the warm end of the cool spectrum. You can only really appreciate the subtle differences by comparing colours side by side. But these differences are nevertheless important, when you come to choosing whether to paint your walls pink or yellow as these large areas of colour will create quite a big impact.

▼ *Wonderful warmth*
Reds, oranges, pinks and golden yellows are the colours of fire and sunshine, of autumn and summer. Use them in patterns and plains to warm a bleak room or make a large room seem cosy.

▲ Peachy pink for a bathroom
Subtle shades from the warm side of the spectrum combine to create a pretty and cosy bathroom. Peachy pink above the chair rail and on the ceiling is teamed with a sandy shade below, and pale cream gloss on the woodwork. These sand and cream shades are picked up in the marble-effect floor tiles. Deep pink towels and drapes at the window add a splash of colour.

▼ Rich rust in a traditional kitchen
Rust-red gloss paint has been applied over anaglypta wallpaper to create a kitchen which is warm, comfortable and evocative of times gone by. The rich colour of the walls works particularly well with the dark wood kitchen units and terracotta floor. Pretty arrangements of dried flowers and grasses pick up the warm autumnal theme.

▲ A cheerful floral living room
Some of the most successful schemes combine both warm and cool colours. In this comfortable and colourful family room, the floral upholstery combines warm peaches, oranges and pinks with touches of blues and green. The sand-coloured walls provide the perfect background for the vivid colours of the painting over the mantelpiece and the collection of blue and green china with splashes of red.

What warm colours do

In their brightest manifestations, warm colours are brilliant and exciting, while in their more muted forms they create a sense of richness and warmth. The palest shades – the pinks, peaches and primroses – bring a subtle touch of warmth to any scheme. Warm colours advance towards you while cool colours recede. These qualities are exploited by interior designers. If a room feels big and unfriendly they use a colour from the warm side of the spectrum to draw the walls in to make the room seem smaller and cosier.

Pink and pink-tinted whites

Warm colours are not necessarily bright or strong. Pink, peach, beige, cream, pale yellow and primrose are all warm rather than hot. They are derived from other colours by the addition of white, which has a cooling effect. The palest pastels are essentially pretty colours, the colours of cottage garden flowers – roses, primroses, stocks. These delicate paler shades can be used to create a warm and soothing atmosphere in bathrooms and bedrooms, or to add a subtle warmth to an otherwise cool and elegant living room.

Shades of yellow

Yellow is a cheerful, summery colour ranging from the brilliance of sunflowers and buttercups to buttery yellows, muted ochres and sharp lemons. As with the pinks there are degrees of hotness, with those nearest the primaries being the warmest and those with lots of white or a hint of blue being the coolest. Lemon yellow and greenish yellow, for example, look very cold when compared with the warmer, golden yellows.

Because of the great range of shades available, yellow is an extremely useful colour with many applications in the home. It can be teamed with green and white to create a fresh, spring-like effect

◄ Sunny kitchen
Sunlight streaming into this yellow kitchen gives it a wonderful, glowing quality, but the warmth of primrose as a decorative scheme would make this a welcoming room on the bleakest of winter days. Cupboard mouldings and skirtings picked out in a golden yellow to match the tablecloth and white painted furniture, kitchenware and floor tiles combine to give the room a fresh, spring-like feel.

or it can be used as an accent colour to bring zest to a subdued scheme. A deep yellow ochre, or an old gold would create a dramatic impact in an entrance hall, while a pale primrose could be the basis of an elegant and comfortable living room scheme.

Too much of one thing can be tedious, however, so a combination of warm and cool colours can be used to create interesting but harmonious schemes. Primrose with grey is a particularly pleasing combination. If your living room is large and sunny, you could consider a true, singing yellow and team it with touches of its complementary blue – colours taken from nature, cool summer skies with the warmth of the sun.

In the kitchen you'll find that cool colours work best with pine finishes while peachy colours and soft yellows work well with woods like ash which have a greyish tinge.

Yellow is a glorious colour to wake up to, especially if your room has a southerly or easterly aspect which catches the morning light. Sunlight pouring into a yellow room has a wonderful, glowing quality.

▲ Warm colours with cool touches
In this inviting room warm colours combine with cools to create a harmonious and satisfying effect. The buttery yellow walls and pink curtains and cushions are balanced by the sharp green of the sofa fabric and the cool grey carpet.

▲ A little goes a long way
The primaries are such strong colours that they always attract the eye. This yellow vase draws attention to the cast iron fireplace.

▲ *Focus on flowers*
An austere room can be cheered by introducing just a single splash of warm colour. Here, an arrangement of fruit, hydrangeas and anemones creates an interesting and colourful feast for the eye which will brighten a dark corner.

Rich, floral pinks

Pink is an extremely varied and useful colour, ranging from the palest almost whites through to warm rosy tints. Pale pinks are lovely for bedrooms: soothing yet warm, they combine cosiness with a frivolous prettiness. In the country bedroom they are most often used in combination with floral and sprigged wallpapers and furnishing fabrics.

The particular shade of pink you use will depend on how much, and what kind of light the room gets. A south-facing room with big windows can take a pale, cool pink with a hint of blue; while a north-facing attic room with small windows will need a warmer carnation pink. A pink that looks bright and cheerful in sunlight can look dreary and washed out in a cold northern light.

Warming a cool room

If you have used a pale pink on the walls and decide that the room is not warm enough, there are several things you can do. As the window is the light source for much of the time, choosing a warm colour for the curtains will flood the room with warm light.

If your existing curtains are in a cool colour, warm them up with a trim in a warm colour. Used along the leading edge of the curtains it will be seen against the light bringing a warm note into the room. After dark, strong, warm colours used for lampshades will bring a rich glow to the room and as a final touch, rugs and cushions in warm tones can be scattered about.

SEA AND SKY COLOURS

Along the shores of the Mediterranean white-washed houses sparkle in the sun, their doors and window frames picked out in intense blue or turquoise. Combined with white, blues, greens and bluey-greens are the main decorative colours, both inside and out. Their coolness provides a welcome contrast to the heat of the sun.

In cooler climates cool colours must be used with care. Sharp whites and blues can look garish in a pale northern light, but a bluey white, or a broken, pearly grey will look wonderful.

Sea and sky colours vary in coolness, with most blues and turquoises being fairly cold, but with greens and purples ranging from cold to almost warm. Those at the warm end of the purple spectrum contain a lot of red, while warm greens contain either red or ochre. Look at a paint manufacturer's colourchart swatch to see where you would draw the line between the warms and cools.

▼ Cool and sophisticated
Blues, greens, turquoise and certain purples are described as cool colours. In nature these are the colours of sea and sky, bluebells and grass, shady woodland walks and heather covered hills. In your home, they will make your rooms appear larger and cooler: you can use them to create a tranquil effect in a busy living room, or kitchen, or simply to balance a room where warm colours predominate.

The qualities of cool colours

Cool colours appear to move away from the viewer. For example, if a block of red paint and a block of blue paint are placed side by side, the blue will seem to be further away. This characteristic can be exploited to make a small room seem larger and airier. If you have a living room which is smaller than you would wish, consider using shades of blue or green to 'push back' the walls.

However, the need to make a room look larger has to be balanced with other factors, such as the aspect of the room. If your room faces north, painting it a strong shade of blue will make it seem very cold, so you could try a paler shade of blue or green and add dashes of a warm colour elsewhere in the room. Yellow blinds or curtains would give a sunshine glow to a room with pale blue or green walls. In a south-facing room with lots of light – a room with french windows opening into the garden, for example – you can be bolder in your choice of colour. A good apple green would pick up the freshness of the garden foliage, creating an airy and spacious feeling, while the light flooding in makes the room inviting.

▼ *Moody blues*

A living room with a very cool feel, created by using related shades of grey, green and blue. Warmth comes from the sunlight filtering through unlined curtains, and from the pink of the cushions and the sofa piping.

◄ Working with blue

A room's colour scheme is often built around one large item – a sofa, for instance, or the existing carpet or a favourite rug – carefully teaming or matching all the other items. With blue, however, you will be surprised at the extraordinary number of shades that will quite happily mix with one another. Here there are blues ranging from the dull navy on the ikat table-cloth, to the slaty-blue of the sofa, the delft and prussian blues of the china, cornflower blue on the gingham cushion and the wonderful jewel-like royal blue of the glasses.

◄ A southerly aspect

A room with plenty of light from the south or the west can well afford a cool blue treatment. Here, the ceiling mouldings and french windows are painted the same strong blue as the walls, but the effect is cleverly softened by painting the ceiling a soft shade of pink. Wooden furniture and rich, mahogany-stained floorboards give the room a warm glow.

► Pale and pretty

Soft light floods through the net curtains to reveal a delicately pretty room with a pale blue theme. The walls and the Lloyd loom chair are painted in a light grey-blue, while the Indian rug is in rather more intense shades of blue and grey. Blue and purple are the dominant colours on the appliquéd table-cloth, and the plant was chosen for its blue flowers. Warm accents are provided by the small vase of sweet peas, and the pinks and reds of the painting.

◄ Bathtime blues

Sea and sky colours seem particularly appropriate in bathrooms, where, teamed with white, they look very fresh and clean. Blue will also make a small bathroom look larger, but before you decorate, check where the natural light comes from; if it is northerly, it will make your bathroom seem cold. Here the clean functional lines of the bathroom suite are softened by pretty swagged curtains, and tiling with a shell motif.

Living with cool colours

People tend to divide into two groups in the decorative schemes they prefer: those that go for the cool, spacious feel of sea and sky colours, and those that prefer the warmer, cosier look of sunrise and sunset. Cool colours are soothing and restrained, elegant and grown-up. They are ideal for living rooms and studies, rooms in which you work and rooms in which you relax. Fresh cool colours make a kitchen light and airy, but in a bedroom they are used most effectively in a balanced combination with warm colours rather than completely on their own.

▼ Going for green
Make a small bedroom look bigger with light, fresh green walls and ceiling with the woodwork picked out in white. Add lots of warm, pretty details in pink and apricot.

▶ Making a point
Glossy dark greens, like strong reds, make a dramatic impact but they should be used in small amounts. A green jug, candlesticks and a bowl of hyacinths wake up a grey marble slab.

▲ **Kitchen choice** *Both blue and green work well with white and these crisp colour combinations look particularly good in kitchens, especially where the stove and other hardware is white.*

▼ **Green peace** *Pastel shades of green give a bedroom a particularly tranquil, airy feel. Here the green walls and table-cloth are complemented by apricot pastels in the cushions, lampshades and quilted bedspread.*

Green alert

We have a strong tendency to associate green, in all its numerous shades, with the outdoors, plant life and the countryside. But, while it is a beautiful and flexible colour it can also be difficult to handle.

The paler shades are fairly safe, and will work in most rooms, but you should take special care with some of the others. Some of the sharp yellowy greens, for instance, can look very acidic, and bright leafy greens, though seductive, should be used in moderation. The vivid green from a pretty floral print can look disastrous on paintwork and walls, though it may well look charming as a bright accent on cushions or tiebacks. If you go for impact and choose a strong, dark green wallpaper for the hall or a study, temper it with rich red oriental-style rugs, or it will have a tendency to look gloomy in daylight.

The easiest and most popular greens are those that have been tempered with a warm colour – these are generally the softer, more muted shades like olive, sage and pale avocado. So use bright and dark greens sparingly, in patterns or as accent colours balanced by other strong colours. And if you naturally incline towards greens, choose paler shades or warmer tones and take care to soften them with their complementary reds and oranges.

Taking the chill off

People generally find it difficult to decide whether a green or a turquoise is cool or warm when they see it on its own – it is much easier to see 'warmness' or 'coolness' if there is something to compare it with. Thus a green room accented with blue will be cool; but if your accent colour comes from the opposite side of the spectrum, it will be transformed into a warm room.

▲ Complementary
Turquoise's complementary colour, a lovely orangey-ochre, brings out all its potential warmth. The beech-coloured pot and the bright cloth make the perfect complement for a turquoise chest.

▼ Autumnal accents
A cool jade green is warmed by lavish autumnal curtains, a theme echoed in the cupboard's darker tones. The bright green duvet cover can take the brighter orange of the cushions.

PASTEL COLOURS

These are the colours of ice-cream, sugared almonds and blossoming fruit-trees. They are pale and attractive, bringing to mind the blues, pinks and yellows of old-fashioned cottage-garden flowers like delphiniums, larkspur and lupins. Even the names of the pastel palette are wonderfully evocative – sugar pink, Wedgwood blue, pistachio green, primrose yellow, apricot and soft turquoise.

These attractive, frivolous colours came into their own in the early eighteenth century when the overblown grandeur of the baroque gave way to the style known as rococo which was fresh, free, airy and elegant. Favourite colours – often used in striped wallpapers of the period – were pale and subtle pastels.

Pastels as a background colour

These are useful background colours they never jar and can be spiced up with splashes of another colour. They are ideal for large areas like walls or floors when you don't want the colour to dominate, yet you want to introduce a positive rather than a neutral colour.

Pastels are mixed from white and one of the primaries or secondaries which accounts for a slight chalkiness in their appearance. It also means that they look particularly good with white. In bathrooms a combination of pastel blue or pink with white fittings and tiles looks fresh, clean and attractive. For a child's bedroom, sponged, plain or wallpapered walls in primrose yellow can be teamed with a yellow and blue sprigged design on a white background

Pastels in large quantities, or over large areas, can look rather too sugary. Equally, because of their high white content pastels can feel a little cool so warm them with earth colours or muted tones. Instead of putting sugar pink with a pastel green like pistachio, try combining it with sludgy olive and beige – the effect will be much more interesting. Other fresh combinations are Wedgwood blue and ochre, pastel green with warm grape and grey-lilac.

▼ Pastel colours
Pastel colours are made by mixing colours with white – red and white become pink, green and white become apple green, yellow and white become primrose

Pastel patterns

Pastels are often used in patterned wallpapers and fabrics, particularly those with floral motifs. However. on close inspection you'll probably find that there is less pastel in a particular pattern than you thought at first. This is because designers have found that slightly muted versions of colours are actually easier to work with than true pastels. However. these predominantly pale and subtle patterns are well suited to the country look. For instance, used in bedrooms they are restful and easy-on-the-eye, but be careful – pastels plus frills might be too feminine for most men.

For a child's room try soft voile sheers spotted with pink or pale turquoise, and delicately flowered curtains. Add a deep pink carpet – crushed raspberry – and furniture stained a sea green.

Pastel looks

There are many pastel 'looks'. The first uses large areas of flat colour and teams it with white for a crisp clean look. The second again uses large areas of flat colour but teams the chalky pastel colours with muted tones and uses a variety of 'distressed' and textured finishes, an approach typified by the Scandinavian look. The third way of using pastels combines lots of pastel prints and patterned chintzes to create an attractive, country-cottage look.

One of the prettiest looks derives from the rococo style – it combines light and delicate decoration in soft tones with lots of white and cream, pictures of pink cherubs and floating clouds. This will look attractive in an elegant sitting room, and for a really sophisticated look, add touches of 'antique' gilt, on picture frames and mirrors, for example.

▶ Playing with pastels
The palest of pastels in yellow, pink and blue have been used to lighten and brighten this long thin hall. The effect could have been sugary, but the dark red stencilling, and the muted colours of the detailing on the cornices and the ceiling rose give the arrangement the necessary edge.

▼ Patterns in pastel
Pastel floral wallpaper, curtains and upholstery fabric teamed with warm pine furniture give the dining room a cosy country look.

White with a hint of . . .

Paint manufacturers have developed a whole range of pastels from almost white through various pale shades to sweet pea colours. These look wonderful in some parts of the home, however try to avoid filling the whole home with off whites as they can start to look dull.

Unusual colour combinations

Don't always go for the most predictable colour combinations – try powder pink and pale straw, pale lilac and pale gold. For a faded country house look add touches of distressed gilding on wooden frames, curtain poles, and even pick out details on woodwork such as architraves or fireplace surrounds.

▲ Childish delights
Pastels have always been
firm favourites for
decorating young
children's rooms; a pink
and white candy-striped
canopy, a flowered
bedspread in baby blue, a
handkerchief lampshade
in primrose, and pink
painted furniture, make
this a delightful room for
a little girl.

▼ Mature pink
The different shades of
pink on the walls and
ceiling look wonderfully
clean and fresh with white
paintwork, white curtains
and crisp white linen
bedclothes. The black and
white fireplace and tiles
and the wonderful, but
unusual bedside table
give the overall scheme
emphasis.

Pastels with wood

Pastel shades work well with some
woods – but not all. Light woods like
new pine and bleached woods can make
the whole room look pale with pastel
colours – this can be avoided by adding
a bright picture or rug. However, this
combination of pale wood and pastels
can be attractive and appropriate in a
young child's bedroom, for example.

Similarly, the combination of limed
woods and pastels might be displeasing.
if it is found in particularly large
quantities, as they both have the same
rather chalky look – limed woods look
much better with colours which have
less white in their make-up, such as
terracotta, olive and old gold.

Pastels tend to look wonderful with honey-coloured woods like oak, yew, old pine or natural oiled oak – try them with cool colours like Wedgwood blue or sea foam green.

Cane and pastel shades are a particularly happy combination giving a light, airy look – with touches of white or cream this is ideal for conservatories or living rooms which lead on to a garden. If you have dark woods like mahogany in your home, select from the warmer side of the pastel palette – go for sugar pinks or try using warm apricots.

Pastels with black

For a really alluring and dramatic Art Deco effect, combine pastel shades with black. Try combinations such as primrose or eau-de-nil (greenish-blue) and black, or pale apricot, cream and black. Add chrome fittings – taps, shelves, towel rails and rings. Choose lacquer black frames for mirrors and picture frames, and add details such as fine black lines on walls and doors. Black or grey marble adds to the Art Deco effect, so think about marble-type worktops.

Pastels for children

When a new baby is expected there is a great temptation to decorate the newcomer's room in 'appropriate', theme wallpapers, with lots of bunnies or teddies in fresh pastel colours which you will want to change as the child grows up. A more economical approach is to use natural fabric and tones which can easily be accessorised and dressed up to suit the child's age.

For a new baby you can create an attractive room by dressing the window with yards of frothy muslin looped up and tied with lots of ribbons. Wash walls with a sponged pastel emulsion/ latex paint – this won't cost much and can be changed later. Keep the furniture to light pine or bleached oak, and add china handles decorated with floral motifs – these can be changed to primary colours to suit a child's developing colour sense. Stained floorboards and cotton rugs will be fine until baby is crawling – then invest in carpet with a small patterned motif – or perhaps carpet tiles which you can replace easily when the inevitable spills happen.

▲ Pastel, neutral and black

A delightful combination for the kitchen is sponged primrose walls, with cupboards and paintwork dragged in a pale grey. These colours are repeated in the sprigged floral curtains and the wallpaper border. Touches of gold on the picture frames make them stand out from the wall. But it's the touches of black in the floor tiles and in the charming fat pig on the cupboard that make the scheme really special.

EARTH COLOURS

This rich and spicy palette of colours is mainly derived from naturally occurring pigments and was used by our ancestors before the dawn of recorded time. The very first time a human being made a deliberate mark on a surface it was probably with one of these pigments - a piece of charcoal from the remains of a fire, perhaps, or a lump of chalk or simply a clod of red clay from the cave floor. Our instinctive need to decorate our homes and to record the world around us is magnificently illustrated on the walls of the famous caves of Altamira in Spain and Lascaux in France, which date from around 25,000 years ago. Here the artists have depicted bison and other animals with deft, swirling lines, filled in with ochres and browns, and the colours of these naturally occurring pigments are still visible despite the time that has passed since they were first painted.

▲ Natural origins
Earth colours are those that derive from natural colour pigments found in clays, and their names come from the regions where they were found – sienna from Tuscany, Naples red, umber from Umbria and so on. They are warm, homey colours, with a strong natural feel.

► **Kitchen chic**
Warm terracotta floor tiles, dark oak units and olive patterned wallpaper work beautifully with white tiles and surfaces in the kitchen.

raw sienna

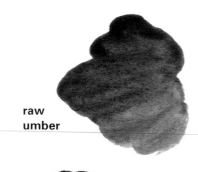

burnt sienna

raw umber

burnt umber

yellow ochre

What do they look like

The earth colours are all on the warm side of the spectrum, ranging from yellow, through various shades of red, brown and green, and including chalky white and charcoal.

They are an important part of the painter's palette, and if you paint you will be familiar with their names which often reflect their place of origin. Raw sienna is a light brown from the hills of Tuscany in Italy. It is the colour of ground cinnamon or nutmeg with distinctly yellow undertones. Burnt sienna, on the other hand, is a reddish brown pigment the colour of ground ginger. The timbers are darker browns originally from Umbria. Raw umber has just a hint of yellow, burnt umber is a dark reddish brown.

The earth yellows are ochres rather than bright yellow, at their brightest the colour of English mustard, but usually more muted – like French mustard. If natural yellow ochres are heated, they produce reddish pigments. This has happened naturally in volcanic regions giving some particularly strong and beautiful pigments such as Naples red from the slopes of Vesuvius.

Of the greens, terre verte is a strong, transparent, true earth green, but for decorating purposes drab and olive greens seem to work best.

Qualities of earth colours

The earth colours are beloved by decorators. First and foremost they are extremely beautiful colours – warm and subtle rather than brilliant, the colours of autumn leaves and oriental spices. They are almost all in the same tonal range, which means that they can be used together with ease to create interesting and satisfying harmonies. Tone describes the lightness or darkness of a colour. Colours which have the same value or intensity tend to produce a balanced, rather quiet relationship, which is useful if you want to give a room a restful or sophisticated feel, or even if you want a foil for other, more dramatic accents.

Earth colours can be mixed with white to create subtle muted shades which are pretty and extremely useful. Individual tastes vary, but some colours can be recognised as 'good' decorating colours – they are used again and again, and always seem to work. Often these colours are slightly off or 'dirty' colours, giving them a mellow or distressed quality. Earth colours fall into this category as they are full of natural impurities.

Look at old paintings, and see how artists use earth colours to bring a blue scene into warm focus, or to 'anchor' a cream or pink one.

▲ A warm glow
Red and white paper can look pink and washy; here it is enhanced by the dark stairs and a terracotta floor. White lace adds a crisp accent.

▼ Earthy tints
A touch of ochre and sienna on the walls and woodwork make the perfect bedroom background.

Using earth colours
Earth colours are ideal for the country look – they have the functional, no-nonsense, rather puritan feel that goes with natural materials and chunky textures. They can be used to create a rustic look, but they can also look elegant and understated in the right setting teamed with antique furniture.

Earth colours with white
Earth colours look best if a contrast of tone or colour is introduced into the scheme. White, either a brilliant white, or a creamy white, set them off wonderfully. In a bedroom, for example, putty coloured walls would look wonderful teamed with white woodwork and white lace on the bed.

Dark brown or burnt sienna set off by white looks particularly smart. A kitchen floor of terracotta tiles and natural wood units will look fresh and functional if teamed with white tiled or painted walls.

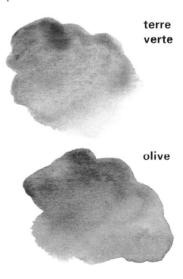

terre verte

olive

▲ Earthenware
The warm natural colours of pottery and earthenware are perfect against the unpainted brick and warm wood of this country kitchen.

◄ Accent blue
The lovely subdued earthy colours in this dining room are beautifully balanced by the splashes of a rich, autumn beech leaf orange, and a faded, chalky blue.

Ochres with cools

The yellow earth colours also benefit from being teamed with cool shades. Try yellow ochre with Chinese blue – an elegant and subtle version of the Provençal combination of bright blue and yellow. For a particularly pleasing colour scheme, use the restful blues for the furniture, with touches of honey tones for warmth. Use pale yellow ochres for the light sources – for lampshades and window treatments – and bring them all together in a Chinese rug in delft blue and ochre on a cream background.

Ochres with browns

Walls painted in a yellow putty shade are traditional in the English country farmhouse. Teamed with polished wood, slate, earthenware and richly coloured rugs they combine to create a restful scheme into which accent colours such as a bright golden yellow can be introduced.

◄ Mellow harmonies
A perfect demonstration on how well the earth colours can be used together – stone flagged floor, parchment-coloured walls, stencils in sepia and tan, and an old Persian rug in brick red and dark brown.

▲ Balancing tricks This salmon pink coloured wallpaper needs the blue and white flowers to balance its warmth; there are further cooling touches of blue in the carpet, cushions and lamp, the touches of wood enhance the overall effect.

Brown earths with cool colours

In design, contrasts often balance a scheme. For this reason, warm colours benefit from the introduction of a cool colour and vice versa.

A cool blue-grey is a useful foil for rich reddish browns. A room with rich, earth-coloured soft furnishings will benefit from cool grey walls. Alternatively, warm brown walls will need lightening with an accent colour such as pale china blue.

In a sitting room try a grey sofa piled high with ochre and russet cushions, with an Indian carpet on the floor echoing all three colours.

In a kitchen terracotta teams well with slate grey and pale blue-grey paintwork.

In the dining room you can afford to go for a more drama than elsewhere in the home. For a really sumptuous effect, try rich rust and brown print curtains and upholstery, a russet tablecloth and a Tiffany shade in a similar range of colours. Finally add wooden Venetian blinds, a polished wood floor and furniture in mellow old woods. Earth colours can be rather dark, so make sure there are plenty of warm pools of light.

◄ Bedroom bliss
This cool grey bedroom with its stripped floorboards is brought to life by the earthy colours of the bed linen in onion-skin red, olive, cinnamon and teal.

▲ Cinnamon and chocolate
This spicy gingery cinnamon, balanced with touches of chocolate brown is perfect for kitchen tiles, a lovely background for wood, glass and earthenware accessories.

A touch of luxury

Earth colours blend particularly well with natural wood tones, and with other natural materials like cane and raffia, sisal matting. stone and slate. The rather plain and functional feel of these materials and colours provides a wonderful foil for a little splash of unexpected luxury. So why not try white lace curtains inside chunky tweed drapes in grey and brown. Or create a simple but dramatic effect by enlivening a basically rather plain bedroom – grey walls and a rich brown carpet – with lots of white frilly bed linen.

The classic plainness of the background suits traditional furniture in dark woods but because these earth colours have a solid feel, you can also afford to indulge in one or two extravagantly flamboyant touches. For example, in a room in any of the colourways described above you could add an elaborately carved and gilded mirror above the fireplace or gilded wall lights. You'd expect to see lavish accessories such as these against a more obviously opulent colour – crimson. purple, glossy peacock green or blue for example – so the effect is heightened by its unexpectedness.

▲ A touch of gilt
To the simplicity of earth colours, add a splash of luxury with ornate gilded wall lights and a marble bust.

▶ Hearth and home
Warm terracotta walls and an open fire, crowded bookshelves and easy chairs produce an infinitely cosy living room.

▼ Country clutter
Earth colours are very relaxing and easy to live with – colours that encourage reading, sewing and cosy fireside chats.

NATURAL NEUTRALS

Nature is the richest source of the subtle and infinitely varied shades that make up the neutral palette. From the seashore we can select the pearly pinks and pale ochres of seashells, the muted greys, beiges and softest browns of a pebble beach, or the sparkling whites and yellows of the sandy shore.

Inland we find the warm greys of granite, the bluer greys of slate and limestone, and the buffs and beiges of sandstones. From field and hedgerow we can take the tawny shades of straw and sun-bleached grasses, autumn leaves and sawn wood.

Technically, neutrals are the shades without colour: black, white and all the greys. To these, interior designers have added beiges, fawns, taupe, stone, putty, biscuit, sand, camel, buff, mushroom, khaki – a myriad evocatively named subtle shades almost exclusively drawn from the colours of nature.

Neutrals have two outstanding characteristics – they can be used together to create satisfying and harmonious relationships, and they can also be used with strong colours from other groups without creating a clash.

▲ Natural harmony
The great charm of neutral colours is their compatibility with each other and with virtually all the other colours. They make quiet, undemanding backgrounds for bright primaries, or rich berry colours, or cool blues and earthy browns. Used on their own, or accented with grey or black, they look costly and uncluttered.

56

Neutrals with other colours

Neutrals can also be used to great effect with other colours. The neutrals may be the main colour or the background colour. You can, for example, enliven the gentle harmonies of a predominantly neutral look with splashes of accent colour. Alternatively, you can use neutrals to act as a foil for a vivid colour scheme.

Neutrals are easy to work with so it shouldn't be difficult to find colour combinations that please you. Don't always go for the most obvious – experiment.

Greys are easy to use, but need to be sparked up. Try primrose as a second colour, with rust as an accent. Or team it with rust and a touch of eau-de-nil (a light greeny-blue).

Cream also benefits from the enlivening effects of colours such as ochre, lilac, pale green and cornflower blue.

Beige can be teamed with pale blue, deep blue or aquamarine, with a touch of blue-grey, black or white for emphasis.

White goes with almost anything, but try delphinium blue, sunny yellow, fresh spring green or pastel pink.

▶ **A natural for florals**
The bleached sand walls and the textures of wood and cane make a perfect background for curtains and cushions in rich colours and bright, glossy green plants.

▲ **Let the sunshine in** *Off-white walls and paintwork, and the stone fireplace provide a quiet foil for the singing yellow of the heavy silk curtains, and the vase of flowers.*

▲ **Neutrals with warm colours** *A warm shade of white on the walls is deepened by deep apricot curtains held back with flowered tiebacks, and the elegant button-back chair in warm terracotta.*

BERRY COLOURS

Rich scarlets, crimsons, mauves, purples, velvety greens and golds are the real colours of summer and autumn. They are true country colours derived from the fruits and berries of field and hedgerow. When we use them we can take our lead from nature: in high summer we see them set against the natural greens of foliage in a rich tapestry of jewel-like colours. Think of the contrasting reds and greens of a cherry orchard – the combination of warm and cool colours giving both colours added zest. Or imagine the rich purply bloom of ripe plums, set against the leaf green of their foliage.

In autumn the cool greens of summer leaves turn to warm reds, golds and ochres before they fall. This combination of old-golds, purples and reds gives us a lighter, brighter, higher-key palette.

In winter the berries on the rosehip and hawthorn tree add a splash of colour to the neutral greys, browns and taupes of leafless hedgerows, while holly berries create a brilliant contrast to the deep, glossy green of their leaves.

Jewel colours

Sometimes it is difficult to find the right words to describe the colours we like. Painters have their own specialist vocabulary to describe pigments: for example alizarin crimson is a cool, transparent red, while cadmium red is a bright scarlet. Non-specialists use terms that they know. For example, the range of colours we have called the berry colours can also be likened to the colours of jewels and semi-precious stones – to amethyst, ruby and garnet. The world of the wine-seller can also come to our aid with terms like claret, burgundy and port wine.

▼Berry colours
These are rich, opulent colours – glowing rubies and golds, glossy purples and greens – their origins lie in the fields and hedgerows, in rosehip and hawthorn bushes, blackberries and olives, grapes and pomegranates. They can be used together or singly, as a main theme or to add a touch of luxury.

Warm reds and cool reds

The berry colours include hot and cool reds. The brightest of all the reds is scarlet, a brilliant, lively red without a trace of blue. This is the sealing-wax red of holly and rowan berries, rosehips and geraniums. At the cooler end of the red spectrum are the reds with just a hint of blue – the crimson of strawberries, the pinky reds of raspberries, and the ruby red of redcurrants. The very deepest reds are almost brown or black – the red of garnets and black cherries.

Handle with care

Berry colours are powerful and intense and must be handled with care if they are not to overwhelm a room. They can be used in several ways. Touches of crimson, maroon and purple can be used to add grandeur to a simple scheme, while a splash of scarlet will bring warmth and cosiness to a large or chilly room, or add interest to an otherwise quiet and restrained decor in pale or neutral colours. If you limit the use of berry colours you can achieve a luxurious overall effect.

A berry-based scheme

The secret of a successful scheme based on these rich colours is to balance warm colours with cool. This happens in nature where the cool green of the holly leaf is set off by the brilliant red of the berry. We can learn, too, from oriental carpets – look carefully at these and you will find that the ruby reds, scarlets and golds are balanced by cool, light and dark blues and greens.

Use the hot reds sparingly as a little goes a long way. The cooler reds – crimson and ruby – can be used more liberally. A deep ruby red was popular

▲ Autumn's glory
Sunlight or flickering firelight brings out the full glory of the burnished reds and oranges in this decorative scheme. The sponged walls and carpet in a warm shade of brown match the woodwork and provide a perfect setting for the dramatic colours of the fabrics. The gold framed mirror reflects light in a dark corner and adds to the opulence.

in Victorian times, when it was frequently used in the dining room.

To create a colour scheme based on berry colours start by choosing a colour for one of the main components of the room – a three-piece suite, curtains, carpet or wallcovering, for example. Team this solid block of colour with other items patterned in contrasting colours with a touch of the main colour.

For example, suppose you have a three-piece suite in red. Teamed with predominantly neutral patterns with a touch of red to link them and a touch of blue to balance the red, a fawn carpet with a red motif, curtains in a red, rust, fawn and navy print, and walls in beige with a cream stripe will give a sophisticated look.

A more opulent look can be achieved by teaming reds with other berry colours – with purples, indigo, dark velvety greens and burnished golds – the colours of oriental carpets. These colour combinations look good with ornate and antique furniture, particularly with richly coloured woods like mahogany.

◄ Kitchen colour
Painting the wall crimson behind the open shelves of the old pine dresser makes a feature of the fine display of white patterned china.

Using berry accents

Reds are the hottest, most dominant colours – although some are considerably hotter than others. The brightest of all the reds, scarlet, should be used sparingly. Reds are marvellous used as accent colours, small splashes of bright colour to lift and warm a scheme. For instance, in a predominantly blue room, add one or two cushions in raspberry or fuchsia with a lampshade and a vase of flowers in the same tone. The reds will really brighten up the blue; take them away and the room will look dull.

In an all-neutral room, a big painting with lots of red in it, plus a couple of ornaments in the same shades, will add zest to soft creams and beiges.

Tip

Know your reds

Reds are difficult to mix and match. They can look similar until you put them side by side, or see them in different lighting conditions – then they shout. Learn to discriminate between the reds, to recognize the hot ones like Chinese or tomato red and the cooler claret red.

▲ Sharp ideas

If you have a neutral colour scheme, sharpen it up with some rich berry colours in lamps, cushions and throws, glossy red or green candles, or bowls of fruit and flowers. Copper and brass perfectly complement these rich colours, reflecting the sun or the flickering glow of the fire.

▼ Vineyard shades

A combination of grapey purple and a dark grey green is more usual in clothing than furnishing. It looks stunning in matching wallpaper and upholstery in this sitting room. The accent colours are the gold and black of the picture frames and the tapestry cushions.

Living rooms

These bright colours look wonderful in the living area. Reds and deep pinks are the most popular colours in this context; combine them with touches of purple or blue, or a deep, dark green. If using large blocks of red – a carpet or walls, for example – avoid primary reds and go instead for the slightly faded tones of burgundy, crushed raspberry or old rose. For a simpler, more sophisticated look, choose quieter colours and bold accents.

Red is one of the most varied, popular and easily obtainable of all the natural dyes in the main carpet-making areas of the world, so many Indian and Turkish carpets are woven in lovely glowing reds, from softest rose to sienna. These are wonderful objects to build a scheme around, practical, beautiful and providing a rich palette of colours. If you don't own an original, there are good quality modern equivalents obtainable from most department stores at a reasonable price.

Purples, mauves and lavenders went out of favour for a time, but are now coming back in. They are an interesting range of colours falling between warms and cools and can be teamed with colours from either end of the spectrum. So a grapey purple works well with a cool, clear green, but also can be teamed with warm colours like primrose or gold.

Dining rooms

The dining room is a wonderful area to embellish with red. Dark, powerful colours enhance the intimate atmosphere, and you aren't usually in there long enough to be overwhelmed. Reds look good with dark wood furniture.

If you have stripped-pine woodwork and floorboards, you can create a really dramatic effect by painting the ceiling a rich cherry red and taking the colour down to the picture rail. Balance this with a fruity patterned paper containing plenty of cool greens and possibly some purples and mauves. Choose a bright rug to make an island of the table.

For a more restrained, romantic look, choose a deep inky blue for the walls and warm it up with touches of Chinese lacquer red. Keep the curtains and walls fairly similar in tone to retain the enclosed feel. Lampshades in deep pink or crimson flatter flesh tones and encourage the romantic mood.

Bedrooms

The typical country bedroom is soothing and pretty, and bold, bright berry colours are best avoided. Choose instead the softer colours derived from country landscapes, the pale gold of

cornfields with splashes of poppy scarlet, or the deep greens and olives of summer hedges with crimson rosehips, or even the fading colours of autumn with touches of berry red and damson.

Find a flower print with dashes of red, pick up this bright colour with piping on curtains, but elsewhere use softer colours.

Another approach is to use lots of white and spark it up with rich embroidered textiles. For example, a white crochet bedspread can be brightened up with Indian embroidered or carpet cushions. Paisley bedspreads can be used to make billowy curtains. Keep the walls white, sand down the floors and add rugs or sisal matting.

Bathrooms

Red is a great colour to warm up a white bathroom suite. Introduce it in towels, bottles, jars, patterned tiles and crisp red and white striped wallpaper. Use Provençal prints for curtains, or find red wooden venetian blinds.

Deep plum mixed with cream and beige is an elegant Edwardian theme. A rich green will also look good with

▲ A formal living room
In an elegant country sitting room the striped wallpaper in cherry and crimson strikes a formal note. Here the rich reds of the walls and the patterned carpet are balanced by lots of white in lamps, curtains and upholstery.

cream. A few old tiles from a junk shop can be used for the splashback and provide the colour key for the rest of the room. Many reproduction Edwardian and Victorian tile designs are now available at fairly reasonable prices.

Mudrooms and half bathrooms

You can afford to make a bold statement here. Paint the walls crimson or scarlet down to a honeyed wood-panelled chair rail. Find room for a small wooden shelf and stack it with brightly coloured books and knick-knacks. Drape a deep-fringed shawl in jewel colours at the window. A deep plum or mauve could also be used as the key colour.

For a more restrained treatment. keep the walls white and frame lots of pictures in glowing reds and pinks.

▲ Holly and ivy
The warm dark green of holly and ivy leaves has been chosen to make this large sitting room cosier. The green is lightened on the chairs with chintz cushions, and accented elsewhere with a warm, glowing red. These rich berry colours look particularly good with the fine dark wood of the bookshelves, door and picture frames.

◄ Softer touches
Most berry colours would be too strong for a bedroom, but these softer shades – soft plum for the curtains and apple leaf green for the walls – work well with the darker accents of the moss green carpet and black fireplace.

Kitchens

Red is a popular accent colour for kitchens. It works particularly well with an all-white kitchen and can be used to jolly up one that is too clinical and modern. Some modern units have a red laminated finish, others have red trims on white or beige.

Look for mugs and plates in berry colours and display them on shelves. Hang cast iron pots and pans in brilliant cherry red or holly green from butchers' hooks. Pile baskets with fruit and vegetables in season – with tomatoes and aubergines, plums, grapes and bright red apples. Add smart striped red and white blinds, or cheerful gingham curtains. Pick out mouldings on cupboard fronts, or stencil designs in red or beige on wooden units.

White, glossy green and the glowing tones of old pine are another colour combination ideal for the country kitchen. Warm it up with touches of red or, for a softer, more old-fashioned look introduce plum, purple and ochre in stencilled motifs, floral curtains and pretty squab cushions. Bunches of dried flowers in the same colours will help to bring the whole scheme together.

▼ Mixing patterns
Berry colours are very dark and have to be handled with some caution. You can use coordinating ranges of fabrics and wallpapers with confidence – here the accent of mauve has been picked up and used to paint the chair rail which separates two very different patterns.

▲ A leafy bower
Dramatic wallpaper and matching curtains combine blues and greens with brilliant berry red and autumn gold. The gold is echoed in the warmth of the walnut table and picture frames.

▼ Mellow tints
You can combine lots of berry colours to create wonderful rich effects, as in this hall. Here walls painted in harvest gold look splendid with the rich, but faded colours of the old Turkish rugs.

DRIED FLOWER COLOURS

This is the loveliest, most varied and possibly the least appreciated family of colours. It includes an almost infinite range of soft dusty pinks and blues, delicate grey-lilacs, creams, beiges, pale olives and drabs, faded yellows, pale ochres and golds.

The technical term for the group of colours we have called dried flower colours is muted. These are colours which have been mixed so that they are several steps away from the primary blues, reds and yellows of the colour wheel and for this reason appear dull, 'dirty', or dusty when compared with the pure, intense hues.

It is these apparently negative qualities which make muted colours so appealing to interior designers. In fact the dusty feel of muted colours makes them mellow and interesting. Of all the colours on the decorator's palette the muted colours are the prettiest, most useful and the easiest to use.

What are they?
Muted colours can be created in several ways. If you look at the colour wheel you will see the primaries – red, yellow and blue – and the secondaries – green, orange and violet. The colours painters call tertiary colours and decorators call muted colours are created by mixing secondaries with primaries.

A different set of muted colours can be created by adding black.

Earth colours, which are really naturally occurring muted colours, have many of the same qualities. Both groups have a universal appeal and have been used extensively by different cultures throughout the world.

But though they are loved by the professionals, they have been undervalued in recent times by nonprofessionals who are seduced by the brilliance and clarity of primary and pastel colours.

▼ **Dried flower colours**
These are the muted shades created by adding black or grey to primary colours or by mixing primaries with secondaries. The soft, mellow results are a decorator's delight.

It also seems probable that in recent times we have lost our natural feel for colour and handle it with less confidence, so the more obvious colour schemes become popular, with the more subtle colours losing out. It may also have something to do with the way that we are exposed to the visual world these days. We are used to seeing strong, vibrant colours in printed matter because magazine editors and advertisers use intense colours to grab the reader's attention and to sell their products.

Using muted colours

There are two principal ways of using these subtle colours. The first is to go for an entirely muted scheme, relying on pattern, texture or a contrasting accent colour for interest. The second approach uses small amounts of muted colour as a foil for vivid colours or to calm down extravagant effects.

Muted colours with pattern

One of the delights of working with these soft and pretty shades is the ease with which you can combine apparently unrelated colours, colours which have no relationship in terms of hue. This is because most of them have the same tonal value so that if you squint at a range of them through half-closed eyes, no one colour will stand out. This allows you to design a room in a veritable symphony of greeny-blues and bluey-greens, pinks and purply-reds, lavenders and sludgy greens. The colours will work harmoniously together creating a quietly colourful environment which is restful and easy on the eye.

A traditional living room

To create a graceful room, full of charm and character, combine floral upholstery and curtain fabrics in these pretty colours with one or two areas of a plain colour.

For example, if you have a large room with good proportions, choose a floral chintz in muted ochres, browns and drab greens for the sofa and one armchair. Use a different pattern in similar tones for curtains, which should be heavily lined with shaped pelmets to give that touch of formal elegance. Cover wing-backed and tub chairs with velvet in muted shades of green, and paint the walls a muted blue-green. On the floor a traditional wilton carpet in blues, greens, ochres and dusty pink will add further textural interest. Add crunchy braids and trims and faded rope tiebacks with large tassels. Elaborately carved and gilded mirrors and picture frames will provide a final extravagant flourish – the frames should be burnished old gold.

A country farmhouse

For a more rustic feel, look for a variety of fabrics in these faded, bleached colours. Natural dyes tend to fade with time and acquire this attractive washed-out quality. Search out folk weaves and ethnic fabrics like ikat and batiks which are available in a range of lovely colours and patterns. These will give the room a faintly exotic feel.

Nowadays there are a great many shops that sell crafts from the third world and these are a rich source of inspiration at a reasonable price. These shops are also an excellent source of interesting ceramics, floorcoverings in natural materials and baskets of every shape, size and colour. Natural materials and woven textures work well with dried flower colours, and will add to the rustic feel of the room.

Another good source is second-hand shops and jumble sales for 1930s, 40s and 50s print frocks, which can be cut up and used to make pretty cushion covers and patchworks. They will yield interesting and unusual prints of animals, dancing people or jazzy designs and after years of washing they will have faded.

▲ Easy harmonies
Dusky apricot, leaf green, off white and beige, with touches of cinnamon for emphasis, create a peaceful living room atmosphere.

◀ Garlands of oak
A sand stripe wallpaper is the foil for the blue-green carpet and the strong but subtly shaded oak pattern of paper, border and curtains.

▼ Colour and texture
The soft colours and textures of ancient wooden beams, sponged walls in dirty peach, grey stone flagged floor, crumpled linen sofas in faded pinks, a textured rug and cane baskets all add up to a perfect farmhouse living room.

Muted colours with texture

Dried flower colours, like the related earth colours, work really well in plain, unfussy interiors where interest is provided by textured surfaces and natural materials. They look particularly good used with special paint finishes that rely on texture and a clever use of colour for their impact.

Mediterranean style This approach to colour is an element of many home design styles. You will find it in the lilacs, greys, cerulean blues, warm ochres and terracottas popular in homes bordering the Mediterranean. There, it is combined with the texture of rough plaster, stone floors and rough hewn timber.

Shaker style The appeal of this style depends on simplicity, craftsmanship, lack of ornamentation and the use of a limited palette of muted but strong colours. Their palette includes matt reds and reddish browns, drab greens, antique yellow, and greyish blues and greenish blues. These colours are used to paint wooden furniture and are picked up in textiles, and combined with neutral walls and fabrics and polished woods in predominantly golden and honeyed tones especially maple and cherrywood.

Scandinavian style is a rich source of inspiration for the country look. A love of natural materials and plain surfaces is combined with a tradition of painted ornamentation on walls and furniture. This surface decoration is characterized by a palette of intense but muted blues, greens, greys and straw yellows, together with some strong blues. Paint is applied vigorously in thin, transparent washes, and this creates an attractively handmade feel.

Characteristic of all Scandinavian painting is the subtle texture of loosely applied washes and scumbled colour this applies to washes of colour on walls, base colour applied to furniture, or freehand motifs on both walls and furniture. Intense-coloured matt paint used in semi-transparent washes over plaster, or thin glazes over bare wood result in interiors with a subtly aged but timeless feeling.

Muted colours as a foil

Muted colours are ideal background colours, allowing you to use vivid and striking shades whilst avoiding an overwhelming or garish effect. These colours can be safely used on large areas – for paint finishes and wallpaper on walls, on carpets or flooring tiles, and on curtains and upholstery.

Most of us have a favourite colour and don't really feel happy unless we introduce a little of it into our surroundings. The muted shades allow you to use

▲ Muted bower
Faded pinks, greens and golds on an ivory background work beautifully for coordinating bed linen and wallpapers. The paintwork has been dragged in an attractive sage green, with ivory details.

▼ Dried flower power
Massed in baskets and tied with crisp lace and rich purple ribbon, dried flowers epitomize the delights of colours in the muted range – old gold, faded pinks, sand, wheat, dull blues, purples and ivories.

◄ Muted welcome
Dried flowers used in combination with wild flowers and gently coloured asters look lovely in this hall. The walls, decorated in muted shades of pink, green, grey, brown and blue, echo the floral arrangements.

▼ Blending tones
Terracotta, olive, drab, dirty pink, and sage blend easily because they are in the same tonal range. The colours used on the walls are taken from the curtains and coverlet and the cherry red shades add an accent colour when the lamps are lit.

splashes of this colour as an accent, no matter how bright it seems.

Some of the most satisfying and harmonious colour relationships are between warm and cool colours. So if you want to use a vivid colour from the warm side of the spectrum, balance it with a larger area of colour from the cool side of the spectrum. If you like yellow, try a brilliant cadmium yellow on furnishings and curtains, and balance it with walls and floors in delicate greys and pale olives, beautiful cool shades from this infinitely varied palette of 'broken' colours. Another exciting colour is fuchsia pink although it can easily become strident and difficult to live with. However, used in association with a dusky mauve and beige it creates impact without discord.

Paint manufacturers have responded to the public's increased interest in colour and now offer colour mixing services. This concern with the nuances of colour can be traced to the revival of interest in decorative paint techniques – these demand a degree of skill and a knowledge of technique, but these skills are most successful when coupled with a knowledge of the way that colour tones and shades work.

The cool reds

The concept of hot red is easy to understand, but the idea of a cool red might seem a contradiction in terms. However, all colour is relative, so while a rich burgundy red might look hot when seen against a pale, icy blue background, it will look cool when placed alongside a brilliant scarlet.

Whether a red is hot or cool depends on how much yellow or blue it has in its make-up. The hottest, brightest reds are those nearest primary red, and those that veer towards orange, while the cooler reds have blue in their make-up which takes them towards purple.

▼ Cherry ripe

A deep, cool red – the colour of ripe cherries – gives this room a rather masculine feel without being either dull or stuffy. Because the colour seems to bring the walls in, it makes the room seem more intimate.

Rubies and damsons

For the cool reds we must look to the overblown, heavy-headed blooms of old-fashioned peonies, the blood-red tassels of love-lies-bleeding and the purply reds of plums, damsons and cherries. Add to this the marvellous jewel-like colours of burgundies, clarets and sloe gins or the brilliant colours of gemstones like garnets and rubies and you have some idea of the richness of colour that you can find.

These cool reds and crimsons are more restrained than the hot reds. They do not advance or dominate to anything like the same degree and are generally easier to use in large quantities. They can be vibrant but not shrill; grand but not vulgar; warm but not cloying. They are elegant colours, often used in formal settings and for important occasions – think of the red velvet cloaks trimmed with ermine, worn by kings and queens.

▲ Fruit cocktail

The cool reds are used for some of nature's most mouthwatering fruits – for tasty cherries and damsons, and for blushing ripe peaches.

Using cool reds

The cool reds have often been associated with splendid and palatial surroundings, so they are perfect for a room in which you want to make a dramatic statement, such as a dining room, or study.

In a dining room you could paper the walls with a Regency stripe wallpaper in ruby red, cream and gold, or create a really bold effect by colour washing the walls in layers of reds, starting with rich scarlet and overlaying this with transparent glazes of crimson.

Choose luxurious fabrics for curtains and upholstery: the Regency stripe could be teamed with a crimson damask, lined with cream and trimmed with gold braid, while red painted walls could be combined with curtains in a striped or floral design, or in a rich fabric like velvet or damask in a bold contrast colour such as indigo. Team with antique or reproduction furniture in dark hardwoods, and brighten the effect with gilded mirror and picture frames.

Maroon, burgundy or dark crimson can also be used to create a warm, soothing environment, reminiscent of a gentleman's club. To do this, find an old-fashioned desk with a tooled leather top and a matching swivel chair. Line the walls with bookshelves or cupboards in dark polished wood, and choose heavy velvet curtains in a deep plum red. Finish with a rich Turkish rug and some hunting prints or maps on the walls.

▲ Victorian splendour
A red patterned wallpaper, thick crimson velvet curtains and dark mahogany furniture create a rich, rather Victorian setting. The overall effect is slightly sombre, so it has been given a little lift with a vase of maiden pinks and a gilded picture.

▼ Cheerful choice
Red is a jolly colour which looks particularly striking when teamed with white. It's great for picnic accessories and for celebrations, so it's a nice idea to make napkins and tablecloths in lively red and white. Add red candles for festive flair.

▼ Cool reds

Combinations with pinks

The colours you should choose to go with pink will depend mainly on how bold an effect you want. While pale pink and white are fresh and light, for example, fuchsia and yellow, blue or green can be really striking.

For a pretty, feminine bathroom or bedroom use creamy pink and white, choosing a wide stripe or floral pattern for the wallpaper and curtain fabric. Paint the woodwork and ceiling white and lay a rich pink carpet or rug. Touches of gilt or brass will add sparkle.

Pinks mix well together – you could combine two shades of the same pink such as pale, sugar pink with deep cherry, for example, or provided they balance tonally, pinks in warm and cool shades, like fuchsia with coral or cherry blossom with flesh pink. As with other colour mixes, it's a good idea to tie the two shades together with a fabric, wallpaper or carpet which uses both.

▶ **Warm glow**
Pink looks wonderfully warm when teamed with the colours of natural woods. Here, the combination is used to dramatic effect.

▼ **In the balance**
The bright fuchsia pink of the sofas is balanced by deep duck-egg blue curtains and cushions.

TERRACOTTA

The word terracotta comes from Italian and literally translated means 'cooked earth'. It is used to describe unglazed earthenware ceramics, but in another sense it covers a whole range of wonderful brown earth shades with a touch of red, orange or yellow in their make-up. They range from pale corals and ochres to deep, russet browns and brick reds, and are found as naturally occurring clays.

Since the dawn of time these earth pigments have been used by people to decorate their artifacts, their surroundings and even their bodies. The warm earth colours are present in our everyday environment – as the bricks from which buildings are made, as roof and floor tiles, paving and earthenware objects. They are also important pigments in the artist's palette, with names like burnt sienna or burnt umber.

▲ Sun-baked earths
The many faces of terracotta – from pale, yellowy mustard to brick red.

These are warm, unassuming, back-to-basics shades, redolent of Mediterranean warmth and light, of corrugated pantiles under an unrelenting sun, and jumbles of pink and red geraniums cascading from terracotta pots on sun-drenched window sills.

▲ Mellow and warm
Spicy shades of cinnamon
and mustard yellow.

▲ Colour in the country
Brick colours range from
golden yellow to brilliant
red. Red and green are
complementary colours
which enrich and enhance
each other when seen
together. Brick provides a
marvellous foil for green
foliage, giving colour to a
garden even in the depths
of winter. Here spice-
coloured painted plaster
catches the last of the
evening sun.

▼ All-spice
The joy of these pale
earths is the ease with
which a myriad shades
can be mixed and matched
to create a scheme which
is warm and colourful, but
at the same time restful.
Terracotta walls set the
tone for the room, with
the other colours selected
from a related palette of
pinks and ochres; a few
deeper colours add
emphasis.

Pale shades of terracotta

These are subtle, gentle, take-me-as-
you-find-me colours. They take their
inspiration from the dusty, sun-baked
clays, from earthenware pots and
ancient brick walls, bleached with age.
They are kindly, natural colours, which
reflect the elements – pale and soft in
bright sunlight, darker and more intense
when wet. They provide an ideal
backdrop for the home, blending easily
with other warm colours, and providing
a subtle contrast to the darker, bolder
shades, which include black, glossy
green and even dark blue.

Spicy touches

Paler shades of terracotta look striking
with pistachio green – an excellent
solution if you'd like a strong but lighter
scheme and want to avoid the more
obvious pastel shades. You could, for
example, use a warm terracotta below
the chair rail with pistachio in the area
above. A frieze in a Greek key design
stencilled at picture rail level will help
to tie the colours together. Or you could
simply use straight ruled lines, one
thick, one thin. Furnish the room in
plain fabrics in the same colours, with
the addition of one other colour that

contrasts — perhaps cream or blue. To retain the cool, restful feeling choose shelves, chairs and tables in pale woods like beech or maple. Limed wood also works well with terracotta colours; try using this effect in a kitchen.

You can create an entirely different effect using the same colours, with the addition of black. This will add a touch of drama reminiscent of the best 1930s Art Deco styles. You could, for example, add a thin black line at picture rail level and stencil another design at chair rail level. Choose black furniture or paint old items with black gloss or stain light woods black for a stylish and comfortable look.

◄ A rosy glow
Soft mellow shades of terracotta will warm and brighten even the coldest room. They look best when applied as matt washes of colour. They suit grand rooms, with classical proportions, but look equally good in humbler dwellings. They'll soften a modern home, and make an ancient cottage bright and cosy.

► Pot luck
Terracotta pots age gracefully unlike their plastic cousins. They are stained by the rain and bleached by the sun, and in time, are colonised by mosses and lichens. They are great to collect and cherish.

▼ Classic terracotta
Golden shades of an onion skin are natural terracotta colours.

Terracotta with other colours

Russets and bright brick reds can be used to spice up otherwise neutral schemes. They work especially well with the creamy shades of white, particularly in settings where there is a lot of textural interest. These themes are picked up in many ethnic fabrics, in folk-weaves from South America, on batiks from India and African tribal prints.

Use these warm but mellow shades to add warmth to cool schemes. They provide a marvellous foil for bright blue, blue-green, and apple green. Breathe life into a deep, inky blue with a splash of brick red, or create a soothing harmony with muted greys, dull greens and warm earthy reds.

▲ Ethnic colour
The natural dyes used in handwoven and handprinted fabrics from all over the world are a wonderful source of inspiration for the home designer. The colours are often strong, but never shrill. Here black, ochre, red and cream provide a palette of colours which could be exploited in any room.

▶ Warm and cool
The combination of warm and cool colours is a useful recipe for a relaxing scheme. In this room the deep brick of the walls has the same tonal value as the slate coloured woodwork.

▼ Going with nature
Pale, neutral colours with plenty of texture provide a relaxing and easy-to-put-together background to living. The natural dyes of ethnic fabrics and oriental rugs add colour.

PEACH AND APRICOT

The delicious, warming colours of peach and apricot are popular for interior decoration, and with good reason. Cheerful and sunny, they are easy to use and comfortable to live with.

The shades of peach and apricot which are commonly used by decorators are the pastels redolent of sorbets and ice-creams, and the glowing golden colours of home-made marmalade or honey. These soft and delicate colours are well suited to northern light and are much easier to use than the deeper Mediterranean terracotta. Use them with pastel tones of a similar strength to give a quiet restful scheme – pale blue and soft green are natural contrasting shades, while soft yellow and cream extend the warming visual effect.

For a colour scheme with more impact, make peach or apricot the predominant colour. Add an off-white carpet to lighten the effect or a terracotta tiled floor for more depth.

Furnishings in hot orange, terracotta and contrasting touches of cobalt blue and bottle green will give the scheme some richness.

Peach and apricot blend effortlessly together to create low-key schemes that are ideal for small rooms. Their pale tones make them space enhancing. This mix will also produce a restful atmosphere that is perfect for bedrooms. Add only white or cream to retain the tranquil feeling.

▲ Fitting out a kitchen
Golden light leaps off every surface in this pretty yet practical kitchen. Colour-washed walls and the honeyed tones of the floor set the scene for the fitted units. Polished copper pots add a finishing touch.

▶ Apricot accord
Elegantly draped curtains frame this tiny window seat. The cushions and blind made up in a radiant apricot complement the floral print. Sunlight filtering through the blind intensifies the colour.

Soft apricot

The skin of an apricot is a gloriously golden colour, intense but not strident. Essentially it is orange with more yellow than red in its make-up giving it a slightly sharper tone than peach. In decorating it is most often used in its palest pastel form, achieved by the addition of white.

Bring a touch of the Mediterranean to your home with this warm, golden colour. It works well with cool, contrasting grey, soft clear greens, and clear pale blue, the colour of a cloudless summer sky. Apricot is often teamed with toning pinks and peaches in floral prints.

A sunny kitchen

A good, strong apricot used in a kitchen with a lot of natural light will provide year-round sunshine. Cover the walls in apricot-yellow paint and team with work surfaces and units in white or stone grey. For a decorative touch, stencil the walls with a deep border in duck-egg blue, with a mid-tone of greenish blue. Venetian blinds in white or grey will continue the clean, crisp look.

An elegant living room

Apricot can be teamed with dark grey, white and touches of black to create a stylishly restrained living room. Try colour-washing the walls, starting with deep tangerine and overlaying it with two or more layers of yellow. Leave the wall to dry between applications so that you can see it at different times of day and in different lighting conditions – this will allow you to judge when you have got exactly the right colour.

For a rather formal look, combine brilliant white paintwork with neat upholstery in stripes of apricot-yellow, grey and white. Use the same colours at the window or choose a colour to match the walls and line it with a paler shade, or even buttercup yellow. Polished floorboards with rugs in the theme colours will look elegant, but a fitted carpet in steel grey will look stunning. Touches of cold cobalt blue will provide a vivid and contrasting accent to the apricot.

◀ Range of apricot
On the decorating colour charts, apricot runs the gamut from the palest cream, through a golden yellow to a much brighter shade which is practically orange.

▼ Antique accent
Subdued shades of apricot wash the walls to give a quiet backdrop to a collection of basketware and white china. Cream painted woodwork and lacy edgings complete the setting.

Using apricot

This exciting golden shade looks delicious teamed with cooler colours like apple green, slate grey, and lots of cream and white. Just a touch can transform the coldest of rooms, so if you have a plain bathroom or a shady bedroom, it's a wonderful means of adding comfort.

If a room looks particularly cold, a combination of sunny colours will do a lot to brighten it up. For example, try starting off with cream curtains embellished with yellow and apricot flowers. Choose a fabric in the warm apricot for chair or sofa covers, and top the seats with cushions in plain yellow and orange to emphasize the cheerful effect. A contrasting green or blue carpet would look good in this setting.

Apricot is a perfect shade to use in a small room as it will add warmth while retaining an airy feel. Remember apricot offers a quieter and more cautious alternative to orange.

▲ Wall story
Although white is often used to paint the walls of a country cottage, this soft peach paint gives a more sympathetic background to the flower garden and blends well with the mellowed grey of the thatch.

▶ Pastel spires
Peach is a favourite colour in country gardens, as displayed in this brilliant border of lupins.

▼ Colour story
Peach in all its shades is an excellent base around which to create a colour scheme. It has the virtue of adding welcome warmth where needed without overwhelming the room. Extremely adaptable, it can be as feminine as pink, as rustic as brown or as elegant as cream.

YELLOW

Yellow is a delightfully evocative colour, its many shades reflecting the moods of the seasons. Springtime yellows are cool and crisp: the sun, still low on the horizon, filters through a canopy of tender green leaves on to grassy banks awash with a sea of daffodils. On warm days of high summer, the sun dapples glades bright with buttercups and dandelions.

In late summer, combine harvesters throw up clouds of dust as they travel relentlessly up and down fields of golden wheat and pale barley. Sunflowers adoringly follow the movement of the sun with their huge faces, while buttercups and yellow-centred daisies creep across lawns and peep out from between the paving stones.

As summer turns to autumn, the countryside is deepened and enriched with golds and ochres, russets and reds. Then, in winter time, the days are short and the sun shines weakly across the landscape. This is a time to gather around a cheerful log fire, to gaze into its flickering orange and yellow depths and dream of summertime.

▲ Good morning sunshine
Hot sunflower yellow gloss on the bathroom panelling wakes up the room like the rising sun. It is balanced by a cooler primrose yellow on the walls, which might have been overwhelmed by the stronger colour were it not for its texture which gives it greater impact.

Shades of yellow

Yellow is the most enchanting of colours – it gladdens the eye and cheers the heart. It exists in a huge range of shades and tones from orange through to green, and from hot to cold. These shades can be strong and intensely suffused, like the yellows of sunflowers and dandelions, or tinged with the merest hint of creamy colour – like clotted cream or fresh country butter.

Although a wonderful colour, yellow is also evasive; difficult to hold in your mind and to match. Used cleverly and with care it can warm a cold room, brighten a dark room and add a sunny, country feel to any home. But yellows can go horribly wrong. The orangey-yellows can be shrill and overwhelming and the lemony yellows can be acidic and cold. One of the most striking sights in the summer countryside is the vivid yellow of golden rod. This strident colour illustrates the way in which yellow, used at its full intensity, can strike an intrusive note.

The way you see a particular yellow will vary immensely according to the light and the colours it is placed next to. In a north-facing room, a lemon yellow can look quite greeny and cold, and yet in a sunny room, the same yellow may look fresh and bright. Placed next to red, a hot yellow can look even hotter, and yet when tempered with cool blue or grey it will look just right.

Hot yellows

If you look at the colour wheel you will see that primary yellow is located between red and blue. The hot yellows are those on the warm side of the wheel: they have a touch of red in their make-up and merge imperceptibly into orange. In this

▲ Team with green
Bright yellow and green is a lovely combination, so paint walls yellow in conservatories or any other room with windows looking on to a garden.

▼ Brilliant bathroom
A striped yellow wallpaper, combined with flashes of warm reds and browns, makes this bathroom a great place to relax in comfort.

category we find the brilliant orange-yellow of marigolds and the yellow-orange of sunflowers. Cooled with white these colours give us shades of peach and a range of golden buttery tones. Modified with secondaries or their complementaries they give us a range of glorious golds and ochres.

The hottest yellows are most comfortable when teamed with colours from the cool side of the spectrum. The combination of warm cadmium yellow with cobalt blue is an old favourite, particularly in Mediterranean regions and in the Caribbean, where the colours reflect the vivid blue of the sky and the sea, and the warm yellow of sun and sand. Use these colours in large well-lit areas to maximize their sunny mood.

To see what other colours go with hot yellow, take a tip from nature. The vivid yellow of sunflowers, for example, is balanced by vast stems and leaves in a cool green; the colour of weathered shutters. Corn is cooled by the wide blue sky, while daisies have a halo of white which both highlights and tempers their yellow centres. You may also see other combinations like lavender fields next to corn – a fabulous and much undervalued mix of colours – or even the bright yellow centre of a rose lovingly encircled by pink petals.

Of all the hot yellows, the creamy shades, like the colour of forsythia, are the easiest to use. Orange-yellow is usually too aggressive for large areas, but it can work well on woodwork, and will add a flourish on cushions and lampshades. The creamier yellows, on the other hand, can be used on walls, and will make even a cold room look sunny and welcoming. Balance the yellow walls with neutrals, or with colours from the cool side of the spectrum such as grey, aqua or blue.

▲ Highlighter
The white paint on these chairs highlights the intense yellow seats. It can be a rather stark combination, but the wooden floor and bureau have a softening effect.

◄ In the balance
Hot yellow walls are tempered by aqua curtains and a blue-green carpet and sofa to create a pleasing balance of warm and cool.

▼ Nature tip
Take a tip from nature and balance sunflower yellow with cool green.

▲ Dinner invitation
*Sponged yellow walls help to retain
the character of this dining room by
creating an aged plaster look, and
they have a warm glow which makes
the formal room more inviting.*

▼ Classic combination
*The classic mix of cool yellow with
grey-blue creates a look which is
elegant and easy to live with. The
balance of plain and patterned areas
completes the harmonious effect.*

Cool yellows

These are the yellows from the blue end
of the spectrum which have a sharp,
greenish tinge, and also some warmer
yellows which have been toned down
by adding cooling amounts of white.
They are the light lemon yellows,
primrose, and creamy yellows with a
soft hint of peach.

The cool yellows are rather restrained and elegant, and in many ways,
are easier to use than the bolder, brassier
yellows. The natural complementaries
of the cool yellows are to be found in
the warmer pale blues and lilacs. They
also look lovely with shades of grey. For
a restrained and graceful living room
team lemony yellow with a pale grey,
accented with white and black.

Primrose yellow and bluebell-blue
are a lovely combination for a fresh and
comfortable living room. This is a
particularly satisfying combination of
colours which works equally well in
bedrooms and bathrooms, and will look
fresh and pretty in a kitchen with lots of
blue china. Avoid combining these
colours with furniture in the rather
orangey shades of new pine, but choose
instead cooler coloured woods like ash
or dark oak. These cool colours will also
lighten a dark room and open out small
spaces very effectively.

Pale primrose is a wonderful foil for
many strong colours, especially vibrant
purply pinks. You'll find that some of
the prettiest floral prints use this
scheme. Choose a wallpaper or furnishing fabric in primrose yellow which
includes shades of pink as part of the
design. This will provide a background
against which you can use a riot of rosy
pinks and purples.

For a more 'antique' look, use
primrose as a foil for terracotta and dark
Venetian reds. In a hallway, for example,
you could colour-wash the walls with a
pretty primrose, then add a narrow
border in terracotta just below the
cornice and a stencil in terracotta and
gold at chair rail level. On a stripped
pine floor lay a richly patterned runner
in an oriental or Persian design to soften
the overall effect.

The deeper yellows, toned down
with white, have the look of faded
gold. These are very versatile colours.
Team them with browns and beiges,
and mid-toned or dark woods, for an
understated look. They also look very
good with pale, bluey greys and aqua;
strong slate blues, jade green and dark,
muted greens.

Because pastels have more or less
the same tone they work together rather
well, and you can create a very pretty
room using these wonderful cottage

▲ **House warming**
A perfect primrose yellow gives this house a sunny, welcoming aspect, and when teamed with white woodwork looks fresh and bright.

garden colours. To check that the colours and patterns you have in mind will work, get samples of them all, lay them together in a good natural light, then stand at least 6 feet away and gaze at them through half-closed eyes. If any colour asserts itself more than the others, it will not work and should be substituted for another shade.

The effect of light

Colours are influenced by the context in which they are seen: by the colours that surround them and by the lighting conditions, so always consider the lighting when you are choosing colours for a room. As a rule, north-facing windows provide a cool, even light, whereas south-facing windows provide a warmer, more changeable light.

Intense colours which 'sing' in a bright Mediterranean light, can look strident in the filtered light of northern climes. For example, a good strong yellow, the shade of English mustard, which looks wonderful washed over the walls of a Greek villa, looks rather uncomfortable in the mellower setting of an English village.

To judge a colour, especially a difficult colour like yellow, you should view it at different times of day and under natural and artificial lighting conditions. The lighting in most shops is hopeless for judging colours, so either take the item to a window or doorway, or ask the shop for a sample so that you can match it with the colours at home.

▲ **Spring clean**
The clean, invigorating colour of buttery yellow adds spring freshness to this large kitchen. This is a particularly versatile shade which looks good with natural wood shades and with muted colours like the green gloss on the door.

◄ **Wild one**
Wild primroses add early colour to forest glades and garden borders. Choose their colour for your home to give it the same touch of spring sunshine.

▲ **Checkmate** *Yellow walls and blue and white checked fabric is a cheerful and very French combination, full of rustic charm.*

▲ **Splash out**
In a simple bathroom you can afford to splash out on colour, like this glorious mix of yellow and Mediterranean blue.

▼ **Five alive**
Purple, green and grey mix well with blue and yellow to create a lively combination for curtains and covers.

Yellow and blue

The combination of yellow and blue is a very successful and very French mix. For a Provençal look, wash walls in layers of thinned yellow paint to build up a deep colour. Add plain blue or blue and white checked fabrics for curtains, chair covers or table cloths and team this with lots of wood and other natural materials like terracotta floor tiles. Add white to lighten the effect, and flashes of pink or red if you want a little more colour.

Antique furniture which is too big for some homes, and often considered unfashionable in others, can still be picked up for considerably less than you would have to pay for modern furniture – and it is invariably well-made. Against a yellow background, it takes on an attractively French personality which can be reinforced with cushions and curtains in bright blue and yellow Provençal prints.

In a light, south-facing room mix vibrant blue walls with lemon yellow woodwork for a touch of the sunny Caribbean. Collect odd items of furniture bought inexpensively from junk shops, and paint them in bright, cheerful primary colours.

GOING GREEN

Of all the colours in the decorator's palette, green is the most evocative of the lushness of nature — of woodlands and pastures and leafy wayside lanes, and still pools bright with pond weed. There are the bright lemony greens of new meadows, the bluish-green shades of young shoots and the dark massed greens of trees silhouetted against the ever-changing sky.

Between yellow and blue
The greens are a complex, immensely varied and often confusing group of secondary colours which occur between yellow and blue on the colour wheel. Greens with more blue in their make-up tend to be cooler than those from the yellow end of the spectrum, but their apparent degree of warmth or coolness will depend, in part, on the context in which they are seen.

At the cool end of the spectrum there are the stunning, clear blue-greens and turquoise of Mediterranean seas, the softer, paler greeny-blues of duck eggs and the deep, dark blue-greens of spruce. At the warmer end there are yellowy greens, some mellow and mossy, others shrill – the colour of limes or fresh young apples. There are also the greens with a hint of red in their make-up, like the muted, subtle shades of khaki and avocado.

A colour for all seasons
Nature provides us with plenty of inspiration when it comes to using the green palette. Greens occur in seasonal combinations that provide a good starting point when planning your own schemes. They will show not only the shades of green which go well together, but also what other colours of the spectrum provide the perfect complement.

▼ The glories of green
Green is a fresh, invigorating colour, yet it is also rich and luscious. It's the colour of nature; of vegetables and the countryside and of the seasons of the year.

Spring greens

Spring greens are pale and delicate, or sharp and limey. They are the colours of crocus shoots seen against the rich brown earth and of tender developing buds. They are bright, life-enhancing greens which shimmer over trees and bushes as their newly unfurled leaves reach out towards the piercing spring sunlight. Nothing quite equals the bright acid green of these welcome signs of life – gaze up into the cathedral-like canopy of beech trees in spring, when the filtered sun gives these greens the brilliant sparkle of medieval stained glass.

Using spring green

For a feminine but non-frilly bedroom, combine pale apple green walls with warm sandy floor coverings. Use crisp white for woodwork – skirting, architraves and doors – and add crunchy texture with a roughly woven white bedcover and lacy curtains. Dark wood furniture will give this scheme a touch of elegance, while pale wood, like pine, will give it a more relaxed feel. If you have a hodge podge of inexpensive furniture, you can tie the whole lot together with bright gloss paint – instead of selecting a toning shade you could choose a brilliant contrast like a strong cobalt blue.

Bright limey greens are splendid colours in conservatories or rooms with a leafy aspect because they create a visual link between house and garden. Use stripes or checks in green and white for cushions and curtains, and combine these with lots of natural materials like cane, raffia and wicker for seats and tables, and coir matting on the floor.

Designer touch

The bright lime greens are vigorous colours which can be used to add a spark to otherwise restrained schemes. A predominantly pink scheme can be given a boost with a couple of cushions in a zingy green, for example. This works because it creates a balance of warm and cool shades – always useful when devising a colour scheme. Try the sharp, clear apple greens with earthy reds, russets and ochres, or with pinky shades like coral. Conversely, the slightly warmer, more yellowy versions of these greens can be used with cool shades like lilac and lavender. The brightest, sharpest greens have an almost fluorescent quality and a little will go a long way: a barely discernible sliver of lime green piping around a cream and green sofa will add a smart and lively touch.

▼ Spring clean
Spring greens range from the softest pastels to clean, zingy shades.

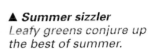

Summer greens

Summer is a time of abundance, when the branches of fruit bushes are bowed low with their treasures. In apple orchards, the fruits are massed on the sagging branches, blushing red as they sweeten in the heat of the sun, and in a sunny corner, luscious red-black blackcurrants nestle against their matt green leaves. Flowers are also flourishing, bright and lively against the green foil of foliage and grassy lawns.

In summer, as in springtime, nature provides us with a splendid source of ideas. From apple trees and roses, for example, we can take the combination of intense leaf greens with splashes of their complementary reds. Use this mix in a living room or dining room by combining a green wallpaper in a period print with oriental-style carpets in rich reds and russets. Alternatively, mix fresh summer greens with cool colours, like pale yellow or icy blue, to create a refreshing retreat on hot summer days.

Leafy greens can also be used in the kitchen – look for reproduction antique tiles in deep glossy greens, especially those with a relief motif and border details, and co-ordinate them with green kitchenware such as enamelled pans and cabbageware pots.

▲ Summer sizzler
Leafy greens conjure up the best of summer.

▼ Leafy retreat
Summer greens look cool and refreshing when combined with icy blues and yellows. Choose this combination for south-facing, sunny rooms, particularly those with a garden view.

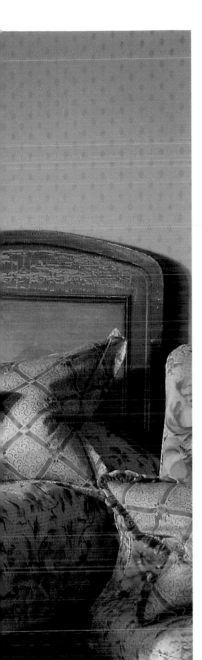

▲ Bright and spicy
Warm, spicy colours, like pink, peach, orange and terracotta, make a fine contrast to sharp apple greens and the bluish spring greens. Here, they are used in a sunny bedroom for a bright, zingy effect.

◄ Cool elegance
Two shades of spring green, used above and below the chair rail, set the scene for this discreet living room. The dark wood table provides an elegant touch, and the striped green and white chair covers have a cooling influence. Note how the braid on the chairs is echoed by the peach in the cushions.

Autumn greens

This is the harvest season of golden greens, when the leaves begin to turn, the colour changing to reveal brilliant reds, golds and ochres. Olive, khaki and avocado are autumnal greens with a warm earthy feel. They are muted shades of yellow green and can be mixed from black and yellow, as well as from some blues and yellow. They are sophisticated and rather masculine.

For a look of timeless, but faded elegance, combine olive greens with golds and earthy reds. Create an old-fashioned drawing room with a William Morris (swirling patterned) wallpaper, a russet carpet and gilded mirrors and picture frames. Choose reproduction furniture in richly figured woods and upholstery in velvets or tapestry.

For a more contemporary interpretation of this colour scheme, colour-wash plaster walls with layers of glaze, starting with transparent yellows and working up to olive greens. In this way you will give the walls a pleasing depth of glowing colour. Cover the floors with neutral or muted colours – natural fibre material or folk-weave rugs. This basic scheme will act as a foil for almost any colour, in particular reds, russets, ochres, mustard and lemon yellow.

Olive green is a marvellously usable colour. Try it crisped up with white or cream, or contrasted with rich navy blue and gold. A combination of olive green, mustard and white would look lovely in a light wood kitchen, especially combined with warm terracotta floor tiles and matching kitchenware.

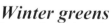

▲ Timeless
Muted autumn greens have a timeless elegance which is perfect for creating a period look. Here, they are used with neutral colours for a very calming effect.

◄ Shades of autumn
These are earthy greens, like olive and avocado.

Winter greens

In a typical winter landscape, bright red holly berries and rose-hips and hawthorn berries add welcome splashes of colour to dark, glossy evergreens. These are also the traditional colours of Christmas featuring leafy garlands, wreaths and the Christmas tree, aflame with red baubles.

Among the dark greens we find the deep blue-greens of fir and spruce. They are rich but cool, intense but not dominating. These are thought of as dark and masculine: colours for the library or study, evocative of worn leather, open fires, well-thumbed books, and rich, deeply polished woods.

The dark greens can be overwhelming so handle them carefully. Use them in places where you want to create drama and impact or where you won't spend a great deal of time – in halls, lobbies and cloakrooms. Enliven the

▶ Deep mid winter
Deep, wintry greens are formal, rich and striking.

◀ Forever green
Forest green walls are mixed with soft furnishings in rich, warm russets and browns for a formal effect which will be particularly attractive under electric light. Use this combination for sitting rooms, dining rooms and studies where you want a striking effect.

▼ Warm and cosy
Bottle green walls and soft furnishings create a cosy look, perfect for comfortable bedrooms or sitting rooms. Dark wood furniture and a bright red lampshade add to the warming ambience.

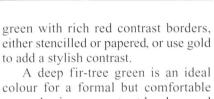

green with rich red contrast borders, either stencilled or papered, or use gold to add a stylish contrast.

A deep fir-tree green is an ideal colour for a formal but comfortable room. Again, use contrast borders, and rich, reflective surfaces to create light and sparkle. Billowing curtains of silky taffeta in a deep holly green would look magnificent hung from an old-gold pole and held back with gold rosettes. A large overmantel mirror with a carved and gilded frame will give the room a really sumptuous feel.

Introduce a splash of scarlet somewhere in a dark green dining room to make the colours sing – a naïve painting, a lacquered pot, or a bunch of red roses will do the trick. When the table is laid for dinner with crisp white linen, sparkling glasses and cutlery, and candles in brass holders, the effect – will be truly splendid.

Living with green

Because green is the predominant colour of nature, it is easy to live with and hugely refreshing. You can find a space for it in every room in the home, whether you add a single leafy pot plant as an accent colour or flood the whole room with its myriad shades.

Nature shows that there is a shade of green which will go with any other colour, so if you choose carefully, you can't go wrong. However, if you aren't confident about using it, stick to something simple, like a two-colour scheme. This may be fresh green with white or cream, or something more adventurous like green with orange or yellow. Remember that it will be affected by the colours you use with it, so use it with a cool colour, like blue, for a fresh effect, or a warm colour, like terracotta, for cosiness.

▲ Something fresh
Green and white is one of the most attractive and refreshing colour combinations. It is clean and light in kitchens and perfect for garden rooms or conservatories where it enhances the plants round about.

◀ Spring sizzler
Yellow and green is a sizzling combination, used by nature in its spring bulbs to get the year off to a good start. Here, a fresh minty green is used as a glaze on the wooden panelling, while a warm, ochry yellow wallpaper is used above. The cool-warm balance which this creates produces a really pleasing effect.

TEMPTING TURQUOISE

The colour turquoise embraces a whole range of fascinating bluish green and greenish blue shades. They fall within that tricky border between blue and green where no two people seem to agree on the precise definition of a particular colour. This is partly because the colours appear to change quite markedly with their surroundings. A 'definite' turquoise can easily become a 'maybe' turquoise, depending on whether it is set against a royal blue or an emerald green background.

The greeny-blues – blues with a green bias – and the bluey-greens – greens with a blue bias – range from the vivid to the extremely subtle. Spirited colours like jade and dark aquamarine are the reverse of the pale cool colours of minty green and greenish-grey of eau de nil and celadon, seen on the glazes of ancient Chinese pottery.

Decorating with turquoise

All the complex and intriguing shades of turquoise are easy to live with and ideal for home decorating. The most intense have traditionally been used to create splendid effects but they are equally adept at breathing vitality into sombre colour schemes.

The subtler colours are kindly; their worn and faded quality provides a comfortable background for furniture.

To locate these interesting colours you may have to find a specialist paint manufacturer or mix your own tints.

▼ *A magical colour*
Turquoise is an enchanting, mystical colour that can transport you from the deep blue-green waters of a coral atoll to the palest, icy green-blue of the polar seas.

Turquoise-blue

The blue of a summer sky has a touch of green in its make-up, reflecting the greens of the earth beneath. Cerulean blue is the nearest colour you will find in an artist's paint-box. These lovely turquoises with a hint of blue in them are a joy to use. The darkest shades are rather formal, the brightest, most intense shades have a bold, ethnic immediacy, while the paler, silvery shades are delicate and refined.

Intense and soothing

The deeply saturated bluish-turquoises are lovely kitchen colours, dramatic yet not overwhelming. Use them as gloss paint on fitted or individual units, or apply them using a broken colour technique, like graining or dragging.

Introduce reds and russets for warmth, in brightly checked curtains, a wood floor stencilled in hot reds, or a bright red oil cloth on an old pine table. A set of red enamelled pans displayed on a high shelf could also be used to add a bold accent colour.

Vivid shades for living

Brilliant turquoise-blue will transform a rather ordinary room into one that is really special. Give the colour depth by building up layers of washes and glazes, or choose a flat, matt paint which will have a soft, rather powdery effect. Used over large areas, this appears as a kind colour which opens up a room, giving it a restful and airy feel. For a relaxed family living room, team it with plump, comfortable furniture upholstered in bold yellow, blue and green florals. For a more restrained and elegant look with a Mediterranean feel, use an assortment of plain fabrics in jewel-like colours.

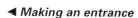

◄ **Making an entrance**
Duck egg blue is a cool and elegant colour. Use it in a restricted space, like a hall, to make it seem larger, or in a living room or bedroom to evoke a sense of serenity.

Subtly ambiguous

The slightly greyish shades of turquoise-blue have a cool, silvery quality which is very useful to the decorator. Duck-egg-blues and grey-blues are favourites in the Scandinavian palette. They are combined with straw-coloured yellows and muddy greens and applied as a series of semi-transparent layers to build up an intense but translucent colour. A variety of decorative paint techniques are often used, including faux marbling, splattering and colour-washing.

The Shakers, too, favoured both the green and blue sides of turquoise, using them as stains on their furniture, to be set against plain white walls and wood floors. Coloured stains can be used to brighten old or new pine furniture.

Dark and formal

The darker, sky-at-night shades are cool and elegant. The green in their make-up gives them an iridescent quality which is at its best in formal settings, providing a foil for deeply polished woods and the glitter of crystal and metals, like brass, copper and gilding.

▲ Shades of turquoise-blue

▲ **Kitchen blues**
Painting the cupboards and lower panelling in a cool Federal blue creates a restrained family-style kitchen with the slightly austere charm of a Shaker home. The russet-red interior of the built-in cabinet provides a rich background for dainty china, while the use of a paler blue draws attention to the scalloped panels of the cupboard doors.

◀ **Gem of a colour**
Painting a wall in an intense aquamarine glazed with transparent black provides a foil for vivid yellow, bright reds, greens and blues as demonstrated by this flower display. The joy of the turquoise-blues is that when they are used in a deep shade, they never become overwhelming or strident. In fact, the darkest shades have a grand, rather formal quality.

Turquoise-green

The greener shades of turquoise are particularly beautiful and evocative. They have always been popular colours, with different hues drifting in and out of fashion at various times. The dark bluish greens of ivy, spruce and the foliage of olive trees were the in-colours at the turn of the century. Later a brilliant jade and the sophisticated Chinese celadon were popular. Eau de nil was ubiquitous in the twenties. Subsequently, colours like pistachio and malachite came and went.

Bright and bold

One of the liberating qualities of these ambiguous colours is the boldness with which they can be used. Take jade as a good example of a scintillating colour which is never tiring. Use it in a bathroom for an aquatic splash or in the hallway and on the stairs for an eye-catching welcome. Broken colour effects like sponging and colour-washing add extra depth to the paintwork.

In the kitchen it provides a lively background for warm terracotta tones and other natural earth colours. Paint cupboards and units in flat, matt jade, or use a wood-graining technique. Team this with quarry tiles on the floor and wooden worktops to create a soothing environment where the colour is pervasive but not insistent.

Pale and elegant

Pale turquoise-green can also be used to create subtle and elegant arrangements. Celadon is a very delicate colour that could be teamed with a pinky coral for a pretty dining room. Or you could use a more intense turquoise-green with a coral red for a touch of Chinese exoticism in your living room.

Verdigris effects, mimicking the wonderful blue-green tarnish of weathered copper, have become popular in recent years. Fake your own with paint on curtain poles, candlesticks and even on furniture to suggest the ageing effects of time while introducing touches of vivid colours. It can be dressed up with tapestry-style drapes, and Arts and Crafts furniture to hint at mediaeval splendours. Alternatively, it can be teamed with stained pine for a more contemporary country feel.

Pale greyish-green pistachio is a particularly pretty muted colour, much favoured in Scandinavian interiors where it is washed on to walls or dragged on woodwork. It sets off lilac, lavender and pinks superbly and also looks wonderfully elegant with silvery greys, dull golds and ivory.

To create a pretty but restrained bedroom with a Shaker feel, combine plain white walls with a chest of drawers, a blanket box and a small chair stained in various shades of greeny turquoise. Throw in a white quilted bedspread and simple, blue gingham curtains to complete the tranquil scene.

▼ **Kitchen diner**
Here, two shades of vivid turquoise stand out crisply against the white walls to create a summery room. Brilliant blue glasses add zest to the vibrant colour scheme.

Cool and watery

To infuse a room with the shimmering qualities of sea and sky, combine a greenish turquoise with a deep cobalt blue. This works particularly well in an attic bedroom with windows which frame the blue of the sky anyway. Put up plain blue curtains, and drag woodwork with a greenish-turquoise shade, including the window box and glazing bars.

The walls could be a textured white, white brushed over a pinkish tint, or a pale terracotta. Sisal flooring and rag rugs will add a touch of warmth. These colours are a joy to wake up to on a sunny summer morning and they are surprisingly warm, especially in a room with a sunny aspect.

▲ **Shades of turquoise-green**

◀ **Shades of jade**
A shimmering shade of jade applied to panelled walls, doors, shutters and even window glazing bars, suffuses this bathroom with cool, watery light. The paint is applied matt and flat which ensures that the room is never chilly. Black and white floor tiles and crisp black detailing here and there add impact, while touches of burnt orange and other warm tones provide a complementary contrast.

▶ **Distressed is best**
A lovely shade of dark muted turquoise-green was applied to this rustic cupboard using matt paint to give the colour solidity and intensity. The surface has been lightly distressed, giving the piece the timeless charm that is characteristic of Scandinavian painted furniture. This slightly greyish blue-green was also part of the Shaker palette and is used extensively for wood.

palest azure to deep amethyst. But for the most lustrous and intense blues we must look to the plumage of birds: the iridescent blues and turquoises of a peacock's fan, the flash of a kingfisher as it skims along the river-bank and the shimmering sheen of a jay's wing.

Warm and cool blues

Blue is usually thought of as a cool, tranquil colour, and it certainly falls on the cool side of the colour wheel. So while blue would not be the ideal colour for a cold room or one with a northerly aspect, it is perfect for a sunny bedroom where its calming effects will induce sleep, or for a living room designed for quiet relaxation.

Some blues are decidedly cooler than others, but it is difficult to appreciate these differences unless you lay samples of different blues side by side. The impact of a particular shade of blue will always be affected by the context in which it is seen, so even a fairly chilly Prussian blue will feel quite comfortable in a light, bright room with lots of warm accent colours, or used in small quantities alongside other hotter colours. With colour it really is all relative – you can only fully experience a colour by seeing it alongside others.

The bright blues

The brightest and most intense blues are those which are nearest to primary blue on the colour wheel, and are neither tinted with white, nor knocked back by the addition of another colour. Nevertheless, when blues are placed side by side you can see that some blues veer towards the warm side of the spectrum, and have a purple bias, while other, equally bright but much chillier blues, lean towards the green-yellow side of the spectrum.

Use bright blues boldly on large areas like walls. For a single-colour scheme choose one of the slightly warmer shades with a hint of purple or red to take the chill off the blue. Apply the paint using a traditional technique, such as colour-washing, sponging or ragging, to give the colour a soft look, ideal for the country style.

Strong blues set off rich red earth tones and spicy shades, the warm and cool shades creating a satisfying balance. So break up walls in brilliant blue with lots of gold-framed pictures and mirrors, and add warm brass light fittings and reddish brown rugs. Accent brilliant blue walls with gleaming white woodwork, and use them as a foil for warm old-pine furniture, or polished antiques in golden or reddish woods.

Bright blue and yellow or orange is another classic colour combination, again based on the balance of warm and cool. Use it with natural flooring materials, such as wood or sisal matting, for a comfortable but stylish room, redolent of sunny southern France, Spain or Italy.

A very successful and contemporary colour scheme combines brilliant blues with jade or turquoise. These colours can be effective when used in almost

▲ True blue
Bright blues are close to primary blue, being bold and lively.

▼ French flair
Bright blue can be combined with lots of white and with natural shades of brown and terracotta for a pleasingly French-style interior which is sassy yet restful, simple yet stimulating.

▲ Splash out
If you're confident with colour then use it boldly, combining bright blue walls with other shades of blue and splashes of warm red and brown.

▼ Holiday welcome
Bright blue is a congenial colour, reminiscent of holidays by the sea, so use it on gates, doors and windows for a welcoming effect.

equal quantities, or with one as an accent colour to the other.

If you want to combine bright blue walls with jade furnishings, you will achieve good effects if the two colours are tonally balanced so that one does not overwhelm the other. To assess relative tonal values, put equal-sized patches of the colours on scraps of paper and squint at them from a distance. Neither colour should appear to advance or recede, neither should dominate. If, however, you are using one colour as an accent, this should be brighter, lighter and more dramatic than the main colour.

▲ Tall hall

Tall, narrow halls are often difficult to decorate, since bold patterns can make the space seem narrower, while plain, pale colours can look cold. In this home the problem is successfully overcome by using a warm, chalky shade of pale blue on the walls, which opens the space out without being cold. A honey-coloured floor and some warm rugs draw the eye downwards, away from the high ceiling.

▶ Soothing grey-blue

Pale, greyish blue is a particularly elegant and relaxing shade which combines well with white, cream and warm pastels. Here, a simple sofa in grey-blue and creamy white stripes blends beautifully with a room decorated in pale blue and neutrals. Pink floral cushions add a touch of warmth to the room.

Pale blues

In many ways the pale blues are the easiest to use, and they are certainly very popular. They are derived by adding white to the most intense blues, so like the bright blues, some have a lavender bias while others are much nearer green. Again, you need to lay different shades of pale blue side by side in order to appreciate the subtle nuances.

These pale shades have many applications. They are ideal for small rooms and hallways, because they really do seem to make the space expand. They can be so pale that they are barely a hint of a tint in white, or a fairly intense, chalky shade.

Pale blue is an inherently elegant colour, ideal for a stylish but pretty living room. This blue can be teamed with other pastel shades – with sugar pinks, primrose and pistachio green. For a pretty country living room, choose wallpaper in these pastel shades: there are plenty of floral, candy stripe and mini-print designs to choose from. Design the room round the wallpaper, using plain pastel shades for furnishings and floor coverings. Scatter cushions, chosen from the various shades, can be used to pull the colours together for a co-ordinated finish.

You can also devise a scheme around pale blue and lemon yellow, although this combination works best in a warm, south-facing room. For a contemporary look, combine icy blue with sharp apple green, adding soothing touches of soft terracotta or dusky pink.

Deep, dark blues

While the bright blues are predominantly cheering, and the pale blues are soothing and refined, the dark shades of blue are grand, even opulent.

Dark blue is formal and lavish – ideal for a dining room which is used for special dinner parties. For a touch of splendour, use dark blue with gold. Choose a deep, dense dark blue for the walls and team these with gilded picture frames and mirrors. Use old gold ropes and tassels to tie back curtains in rich brocades or velvets, and trim other soft furnishings to match.

On the other hand, if you prefer a casual, ethnic look, paint the walls dark blue and lay kelims and rugs on to polished floors, choosing rich earth shades. Collect tribal artifacts – hand-carved and painted sculptures, roughly made pots and any objects with a hand-made quality – and place them around the room. Kelims or kelim prints are wonderful for upholstery.

▲ Smart and dark
Rich, deep, dark blues are formal, elegant and sophisticated.

◄ Rich blue
A deep, warm blue makes a wonderful background for pictures and paintings, creating an inviting but expensive-looking effect.

▼ Blue elegance
Blue-on-blue striped wallpaper is an elegant choice for a formal dining room. Reddish woods and rich golds are splendid team-mates.

▼ Shades of pale
Pale blues are soft, popular and easy to live with. The slightly warmer shades, like these, are particularly effective, being light without being too cold.

Blue combinations

All shades of blue look marvellous with white. While dark blue and white looks striking and rather formal, pale blue and white looks dainty. For example, dark blue is often used to paint front doors on grand terraces, with white for window reveals and rendering.

A pale blue and white combination is great for restful living rooms or fresh and graceful country bedrooms. Combine pale blue colour-washed walls with lots and lots of white – on woodwork, curtains, bed linen and furnishings. Introduce texture by using lace and slubby, natural-looking fabrics or heavy weaves like linen or linen union. For warmth add splashes of a contrasting orange, soft red or pink, and choose furniture in honey-coloured woods or natural wicker which add warmth due to their natural colour tones.

If you are feeling more adventurous, mix the stronger shades of blue with tonally balanced shades of other colours. The blackish blues, for example, work well with rich reds, crimson and terracotta. You could decorate living room walls in dark terracotta, with skirtings, doors and window boxes picked out in deep blue, and curtains in rich blue damask. Dark, highly polished antique or reproduction furniture would look splendid in such a grand setting.

▲ Easy combination
Just looking at a blue and white colour scheme makes most people feel relaxed and at their ease. For a practical approach to this scheme, use easy-care blue and white patterned fabrics and furnishings against spongeable white walls. Floors can be covered with practical, washable cotton rugs.

◄ Jolly jugs
Blue and white is a traditional colour combination for earthenware and it's still popular today.

▲ Colourful kitchen
This large kitchen has been brightened up with walls in a wonderfully deep shade of terracotta and painted units in two shades of blue. Because the dark blue looks best against the terracotta, this is used for the shelves, worktop and window, while the mid blue animates the cupboard fronts.

SPARKLING WHITE

▲ All white
White articles come in many beautiful shades and textures which all look light and fresh. Here, the bright white of the elegant china and soft lace blend beautifully with the natural creamy white of the flowers.

White is one of the most important colours in the home designer's palette. It provides a marvellous foil for other colours, allowing brilliant shades to really sing and throwing subdued colours into sharp relief. It is also used as an accent colour, providing crisp detail, adding light to a dark scheme, and bringing serenity to a colourful one.

There are many different shades of white: warm whites and cool whites; whites with a hint of blue and whites with a hint of pink; creamy whites and green whites. Paint manufacturers are aware of the importance of these subtle differences, and most produce a range of whites tinged with another colour.

White on white schemes first became popular in the 1920s and 1930s, partly as a reaction against the rich or sombre colours of the previous century, and partly as a result of the introduction of a bright and stable white, titanium oxide. The idea caught on and soon

drawing rooms everywhere were being dressed up in shades of white set off with touches of gold and shimmering crystal lights and accessories.

White and light

White has many special qualities. It is associated with light and can make a room look brighter. But take care, it can also have the opposite effect – a cool, badly lit room painted all-white may look even darker and more chilly. This is because white is a highly reflective colour, maximizing any available light, so if there is little around, it will merely draw attention to the deficiency. A more effective way of bringing light into a dark room would be to paint the window frames and recesses white, to direct as much natural light into the room as possible.

Because white reflects light and dissolves spaces, it provides the home-maker with a classic way of creating or emphasizing a sense of space. It can be used to draw attention to the soaring qualities of a lofty room, or to make a small room look brighter and roomier.

▲ Practical
Woven patterns help to soften white and add interest without fussiness. They also make white more practical by helping to disguise any stains.

◄ Timeless
White is seen as a clean colour, so it's popular for bathrooms and kitchens where hygiene is important. Used with a hint of another colour, as here, it has timeless charm.

▼ Bright white
Lacy white curtains are a popular feature of cottage homes. They look bright and fresh as they filter sunlight into the home.

Pale combinations

One of the joys of white is the way in which it can be mixed with other whites, especially textured whites, and with creams and neutral shades.

Try draping a bed coronet or four poster with generous swathes of natural fabrics like muslin and voile; the simpler the treatment, the better. Alternatively, hang plain muslin at the window – for a special effect it can be stencilled with a motif taken from elsewhere in the room. A nice idea would be to fix ties to the fabric and hang it ungathered from an iron curtain rail. Old lace can be used in the same way.

A Jacquard bedspread with a crunchy self-pattern will look fresh and pretty. During the day you could add cushions for a comfortable, informal look, covering them in plain calico, elaborated with pleats or white buttons.

In living rooms white can look arty and comfortable, or cool and elegant. If you favour a simple living room with a rustic feel, combine lots of textured fabrics and surfaces with natural materials like stone, wood and brick.

At the window use sheers to filter the light – there are some lovely fabrics available with dainty sprigged patterns or spots. Look for fabrics which drape well, and avoid brilliant white which can look unnatural. For the main drapes use canvas or a heavy woven wool fabric with an obvious weave. Choose another woven fabric for upholstery and set it off with an ethnic rug in creamy shades

◄ *Tops for texture*
White always looks fresh and bright, and being so subtle, it allows the texture of fabrics to dominate.

▼ *Soothing sight*
An all-white bedroom is a relaxing place to be, but it can look a bit spartan unless there is plenty to see. Here, texture and tone add subtle interest, while the blue flash of a cushion adds colour.

with touches of earth colours, then pick up the colours in cushion covers.

For a grander, more elegant scheme combine whites, creams and neutrals with mirrors, crystal chandeliers and touches of gold. Choose a buff embossed wallpaper, and team this with glossy white paintwork. Drape the windows with a pretty toile de Jouy fabric in cream on beige, or in a delicate two-tone damask, tied back with a self-fabric tie trimmed with gold. The curtain headings should be formal.

Give this setting a touch of luxury with a striking brass light fitting in a chandelier style, and hang prints of architectural or botanical subjects for classical character. An imposing mirror over the fireplace will make the room seem larger and brighter – look for one with classical decorations like swags and cherubs. In this setting furniture should be antique or reproduction.

White with colours

White goes with every colour, but the effects and moods achieved with each combination are entirely different. When teamed with pastels, the result is dainty and romantic, but when combined with primaries, the effect is bright, bold and zingy.

With green

Green and white is fresh and spring-like, ideal for rooms which open on to a garden or have a leafy aspect. The green picks up the shades of the plants out-doors, while the white reflects light and colour. You don't need a great deal of green in a room to create this effect because the green outside will amplify the green indoors.

With blue

Blue and white is a classic and appealing combination of colours – witness the enduring popularity of willow pattern, blue and white Wedgwood, and Delph. It can be used to create a comfortable country-style kitchen, a graceful living room, or a rustic sitting room with a flavour of the hot Mediterranean shores.

With red

Red and white is a jolly colour combination, ideal for kitchens, bathrooms and children's rooms.

A little red goes a long way, so introduce it slowly into a white room scheme. Use it to show off furniture in pale woods like pine, or laminates in cream or grey. Add further interest to the room with touches of cool, dark blue or green to balance the hot red.

With yellow

Of all the combinations with white, yellow and white is probably the most elegant. In a sunny white drawing-room or bedroom, primrose yellow curtains will look wonderful when combined with chairs covered in a pretty sprigged fabric in several shades of yellow. Try using a very pale yellow and two slightly darker shades to paint fake panels on the walls, or stencil on a border for a classic finish. A practical grey or blue carpet will provide a cool balance.

◄ Wood green
In a large high-ceilinged room, satin green paint draws the eye down to the elegant woodwork.

As an accent colour

White is probably the most popular accent colour. It is widely used for woodwork because it is clean, fresh and bright; and it is also the traditional colour for decorative plaster-work, such as ceiling roses, cornices and corbels.

For an elegant bedroom paint the walls in a chalky pastel colour, with the ceiling in a slightly lighter shade, or choose a floral or mini-print wallpaper with a white background. Pick out the ceiling rose, cornicing and woodwork in white, choosing a satin paint for the woodwork. Then choose a textured white bedspread to draw the scheme together.

In a living room choose a stronger wall colour. Paint the ceiling and woodwork white, and cover the seating in a patterned fabric.

▲ White accents
In a large, elegant sitting room, white paint on the windows and wooden panelling helps to break up the impact of sunny yellow walls, while the blue upholstery provides a cool balance. The effect is light, yet bright.

◄ True blue
Although there isn't actually a huge amount of blue in this room, its effect is dominant because the white walls and stone floor provide such a subtle background. Blue and white china form a link.

► Checkmate
A red and white checked table cloth makes this table look bright and cheerful. The chairs are painted to match, with white seat cushions, while the floral squab cushions pick up other colours in the room.

◀ **Versatile mix**
Black and white is a striking combination for quilting and appliqué work, showing off the intricacies of the pattern to perfection. Since it is such an easy colour combination, it also means that you will be able to use the finished handiworks in any room, no matter what its colour scheme.

White with black

The combination of white and black has an enduring popularity which dates back hundreds of years. In Tudor homes the plaster, both inside and out, was whitewashed between black oak beams. Later, black and white floor tiles came into fashion, and fireplaces were usually black with white or off-white marble or painted wooden surrounds.

White and black are a striking combination, being direct opposites – while white reflects light, black absorbs it. In equal quantities, black and white create an invigorating combination, ideal for an elegant hallway, while an all-white room scheme, with just a touch of black, is classy and understated, perfect for a master bedroom or formal dining room.

A room decorated solely in black and white can look a little spartan, even if the room is sunny, so jolly it up, and soften its harsh lines, with touches of one or two other colours. For a really restful scheme, add neutral colours, like grey, cream or beige, or if you want a more vigorous effect, choose flashes of bright colours, like fuchsia pink, scarlet or royal blue. It's easy to ring the changes by introducing new colours.

▲ **Show off**
White glossy paint looks bright and clean, so it's a popular choice for woodwork both inside and out. It's particularly effective on rustic doors, where it's perfect for showing off traditional cast-iron door furniture. Here, the striking effect has been emphasized by painting the door surround black. Note that the door plaque picks up these colours, and also echoes the clematis over the door.

◀ **Smart choice**
This fresh white kitchen has been jazzed up with a black and white checked floor. The floor looks like it has traditional tiles, but in fact it is covered more economically with linoleum.

Black and white is a good colour scheme for a kitchen because it is unlikely to become dated, and you can change the mood with colourful tea towels, bowls and accessories. It also looks very hygienic.

NATURALLY BROWN

Brown is an all-embracing term to describe a phenomenal range of fascinating colours, from purple-tinged mushroom, through neutral biscuit to ruddy chestnut and dark chocolate. Many of these browns are a very familiar part of the natural landscape and, as such, can play an evocative part in the design of a home. Look around almost any house and you will find a host of browns appearing as wooden floorboards, doors and furniture, quite apart from any painted surfaces, which can feature in your look.

▼ Scrumptious shades
The association between the rich colours and irresistible aromas of, for example, dark chocolate cake and strong 'black' coffee expresses the seductive quality of these deeper shades of brown perfectly.

Dark rich browns

Brown is a predominant colour in nature. It is especially evident in the soil underfoot and the trees in the landscape. The autumn scene provides the richest spectrum of browns – a complex meld of rich, warm shades, regularly interspersed with the deep chocolate ridges of freshly ploughed fields.

The natural world is a marvellous source of inspiration for both colour and texture. Wonder at the gleaming russet of a strutting farmyard cockerel, and the glint on the ginger coat of the prowling fox. Admire the silky richness of the polished grain on wooden furniture, doors and panelling. Contrast the grey-brown, geometric patterns on pine cones with the glossy brown of chestnuts and the greeny browns of shiny seaweeds.

Then recapture those qualities in your decorations at home.

A brown study

The darkest and richest browns, the chocolates, chestnuts and mahoganies, can be extremely dramatic when used on a large scale. They can also be dotted here and there for emphasis, to add crisp detail or as a sharp accent in a neutral scheme. The slightly lighter, spicier shades of cinnamon and ginger bring a warm, zesty sparkle to a room.

Use the intense, dark colours for cosy, comfortable rooms designed for work or contemplation. You can recreate the peaceful atmosphere of an old-fashioned library on a more intimate scale in a small study. Combine wood shelves with sand or russet coloured

▲ **Cool, dark browns**

◀ **Black and tan**
A combination of brown walls and carpet with matt black fitments makes a resoundingly masculine statement in a smart bathroom.

◀ Lambrequined
Chocolate gingham and stripes collaborate in a bold window dressing.

▼ Gingersnap
A gingery colour spices up these walls, making them look remarkably like wood panelling at first glance.

▲ Warm, deep browns

► House warming
Deep caramel-coloured walls generate a warm, elegant cosiness in this room. They also serve as an unassuming backdrop for diverse memorabilia and paintings.

wallpaper. Although brightly coloured modern paperbacks lack the elegance of old Moroccan bindings, you can fake the look by facing them with lengths of simulated leather book spines.

Edwardian comfort

Browns, russets and greens were much admired by the Edwardians. Combine olive-green tiling in the fireplace with polished wood floors and panelled walls, stained or painted to a suitably dark shade. Alternatively, divide the wall horizontally, with Lincrusta below the chair rail and an elegant Regency stripe above. Team a buff carpet with a brown border with chairs upholstered in a cut-pile fabric in autumnal tones.

Sheer luxury

Generally, the dark browns convey seriousness and the earth browns suggest natural settings, but a selection of browns can also create pretty, rather frivolous schemes. Look for glamorous fabrics, like velvets, tapestries and fake furs. In a bedroom, a quilted bedspread in bronze, with lustrous beads, imparts a deluxe feeling. Choose coppery brown for the curtains, trimmed with old-gold braid and gilded tassels.

Pale and neutral browns

All the browns can be blended with white to create a related range of paler shades. Adding white reduces their brownness and accentuates the main colour from which they were mixed originally. So a ginger brown mixes with white to quite a pinky shade, a greenish brown becomes a putty or olive shade, while the yellow browns turn to shades of fawn, biscuit, manila and camel.

The very pale browns, like oatmeal and café au lait, are particularly cool because of the amount of white in their make-up. If there is any blue or black in their composition, the colours will tend to veer towards stone-like grey, taupe, dun and beige. Limed oak, where whiteness is rubbed into the wood's grain, gives a similar impression.

These neutral shades are a joy to use and very adaptable. You can either combine a selection of related shades with a variety of exciting textures or use them to provide a quiet foil for richer colours, including other browns as well as shades of red, blue or green.

◀ Streamlined
This taupe and beige striped wallpaper is striking in its directness. Such a colour scheme could be drab, but used in big, bold stripes it acquires distinction.
Painting white plates to match the wallpaper and arranging them at jaunty angles against the vertical lines proves just how amusing plain stripes can be.

Country textures

The paler shades of brown are an excellent way of producing a modern country look, without resorting to frills and florals. By focusing on different textures and materials instead, you can quite cheaply conjure up a convincingly rustic atmosphere.

Choose related colours but contrasting textures, with just a touch of accent colour. Combine dark glossy furniture with a scrubbed pine table, rough-hewn chairs and a chest. Then lay some natural-coloured sisal, jute or seagrass matting on the floor.

Look out for textured weaves, such as tweeds and berber carpets in oatmeal and biscuit. Calico, muslin and cotton duck can be dyed to a superb range of fawns, taupes, beiges and sandstones. Complement the look with stone, brick or quarry tiles on the walls or floor.

For a more rural look, wash rough – plaster walls with a rusty brown colour. To complete the effect, introduce simple earthenware pots and country chairs with seats woven in cane, rush or rough hessian upholstery tape.

▲ Mushroom browns

▲ *Tawny browns*

▲ Anything goes
*Extremes of dark and light brown
provide a neutral setting for a welter
of colours and patterns.*

▶ Gain time
*Painting textured wallpaper in a
subtle biscuit colour successfully
mimics the dirty yellowness of
roughened plaster that is
characteristic of old cottages.*

Ethnic browns

Both the rich earthy colours and the
subdued, paler neutrals lend themselves
to the popular ethnic look that combines
materials and artifacts from all over the
world. Printed cushions from West
Africa in shades of earth and black,
solidly made carved screens and tables
from India, and rattan, cane and bamboo
furniture from Asia all fit comfortably
in this rustic theme. Alternatively, you
can go for the bleached Scandinavian
look with unvarnished or unpolished
sanded wooden floors, adding wicker
furniture, baskets and a rush mat as
appropriately rugged foils.

Juxtaposing matt surfaces against
shiny ones to suggest textural
differences is another powerful design
ploy. Glossy black or chocolate painted
woodwork against matt ginger walls is
simply executed but makes an
amazingly striking impression. Plain
sandy or beige coloured walls set off
honey-coloured varnished wood to a
tee. Similarly, the soft sheen on silk
fabrics creates a gentle, rich contrast to
rough materials like bamboo and rush.

◀ **Browny points**
Different shades of brown are usually harmonious. Here, sandy, chestnut and chocolate browns are mixed together to create a mellow autumnal colour scheme, with all the richness of a Mediaeval tapestry. The warmth of the wallpaper and fabric is nicely balanced by the blue-green paintwork.

▼ **Behind the scenes**
Paler hues of brown can provide a restrained background for some adventurous decor.
　　These putty-coloured stripes on the walls provide a neutral foil for a series of dramatic effects which depend on the tension between the colour and pattern of the drapes and upholstery and the gold of the mirror.

Brown and other colours

Brown in all its manifestations is a remarkably flexible colour which can work with almost any other colour in the spectrum. The warm, gingery browns are the most dominant. To have an impact in their own right they should be teamed with white or similar brown colours, like the honey-browns, russets and ochres of the countryside in autumn. Use cinnamon paint on the walls, with picture rails and skirtings picked out in a dark tobacco brown. Paint the ceiling and walls above the picture rail in an oatmeal shade for a cool, light effect, or in a camel or sandy colour for a slightly warmer feel.

　　Most browns can also be used as a foil for brighter, more vibrant colours. Dressing them with strong, cool colours like purples and blues or muted greens creates an especially dramatic effect.

INDEX

**Page numbers in *italic* refer to
captions and illustrations**

A

accent colour,
accent colours
  autumnal, *40*
  berry colours, 59
  complementary, *14*
  definition, 10
  red, 74
  white as, 119
accessories, matching colours with, 18
apricot, 87-90
  soft, 89
  using, 89
autumnal accents, *40*

B

background colours, pastels, 41
bathrooms
  berry colours, 60
  blue, *22*, 37
  peachy pink, *30*
bedrooms
  berry colours, 60, *61*
  earthy colours, 47
  greens, *38, 39, 40*
  greys, *49*
  neutral colours *53, 55*
  pink, *43*
beige, neutral colours, 51-6
berry colours, *9*, 57-62
  accent colours, 59
  jewel colours, 57
black, white and, 120
blues, 109-14
  bright, 110-11
  combinations, 114
  cool, 110
  dark, 113
  pale, 113
  pastels, 41-4
  sky colours, 35-9
  turquoise, 103-9
  warm, 110
  white and, 118
  yellows and, 96
broken colour, definition, 10
browns, 121-6
  colours and, 49
  dark, 122-4
  ethnic, 125
  neutral, 124
  ochres and, 48
  other colours and, 126
  pale, 124
buffs, neutral colours, 51-6

C

calico, 54
catalogues, 18
ceilings, low, 18
children's rooms, 18, *43*
choosing colour schemes, 17-22
  aids, *17*
  checklist, 18
  patterns and, 20, *20-1*
  personal preferences, 18
  practical choices, 17
  single-colour schemes, 19
  sources of inspiration, 22
  starting from scratch, 17

ways of, 18
colour
  definitions, 10
  language of, 6
  personality, 5
  recognizing, 5-10
  understanding, 11-16
colour charts, *17*
colour wheel, 12, *12*
complementary colours, 14, *14-15*
  as accents, *14*
  definition, 10
  muted, 14
contrast colours, *11*
  definition, 10
cool colours, 5, 7
  browns and, 49
  definition, 10
  living with, 38
  ochres with, 48
  Provençal, 23
  qualities of, 36
cool rooms, warming, 34, 40
co-ordinated colours schemes, 20
coral colours, 78
country look, 6, 55, 64, 66, 124
cream, neutral colours and, 56
crowded rooms, 18

D

dining rooms
  berry colours, 60
  earthy colours, *48*
  floral patterns, *34*
  terracotta, 85
dried flower colours, *9*, 63-8
  as a foil, 66-7
  neutrals and, 68
  patterns with, 64
  texture with, 66
  using, 64

E

earth colours, *8*, 45-50
  luxurious qualities, 50
  qualities, 46
  using, 47
  with white, 47
entrance halls, 18
ethnic colours
  browns, 125
  terracotta, 84-5, *86*

F

fabrics, co-ordinating, 20
flannel, 55
floor textures, neutral colours, 54
floral patterns, 20
frequently used areas, 18

G

greens, 39, 97-103
  autumn, 100
  fresh green, *19*
  living with, 102
  pastels, 41-4
  sea colours, 35-9
  spring, *98*
  summer, 99
  turquoise, 103-9
  white and, 118
  winter, 100-1
greys, neutral colours, 51-6

H

hallways, pastel, *42*
harmonious colours, *11*, 13
  definition, 10
  grading, 16
  monochrome schemes, 13
  related harmonies, 13

I

inspiration, sources of, 22

J

jewel colours, 57

K

kitchens
  apricot, 89
  berry colours, *58*, 62
  blue and greens, *39*
  earth colours, *48, 49*
  neutral colours, *55*
  pastels, *44*
  reds, *30*, 73
  terracotta, *11, 16*
  tranquil effects, *35*
  yellow, *33*

L

light
  effect on colours, 18
  effect on yellows, 95
  white and, 116
lighting, effect on colour, 5
linen, 55
living rooms
  apricot, 89
  berry colours, 60, *60*
  bright colours, *5*
  cool feeling, *36*
  floral, *30*
  muted colours, 64
  tranquil effects, *35*
lobbies, 18

M

Mediterranean style, muted colours, 66
monochrome schemes, 13
mudrooms, berry colours, 60
muslin, 54
muted colours
  complementaries, 14
  definition, 10
  dried flower colours, 63-8
  neutrals and, 68
  patterns with, 64
  Provençal, 23-4
  texture with, 66
  using, 64

N

neutral colours, *8*, 51-6
  definition, 10, *10*, 51
  floor textures, 54
  muted colours and, 68
  north-facing situations, 18
  other colours and, 56
  total look, 52
  wall textures, 52-3
north-facing situations, 178

O

ochres
  browns and, 48
  cool colours and, 48
oranges, sunrise and sunset colours, 29

P

pastel colours, 7, 41-4
  as backgrounds, 42
  with black, 44
  children's rooms, 44
  definition, 10
  patterns, 42
  unusual combinations, 42
  with wood, 43-4
patterns, starting from, 20, 20-1
peach, 87-90
personal preferences, 18
pinks, 75-80
  bright, 77
  combinations with, 80
  cool, 76-7
  coral colours, 78
  pastels, 41-4
  shell pinks, 78-9
  sugar almond, 76-7
  sunrise and sunset colours, 29, 31, 34
  warm, 78-9
primary colours, 6
  definition, 10
  Provençal, 23, 26-7
problem solving, 16
Provençal colours, 23-8
  cool colours, 23
  muted colours, 23-4
  warm colours, 23
Provençal prints, 6

R

red
  accents, 74
  berry colours, 58
  cool, 58, 70-1
  riotous, 69-74
  sunrise and sunset colours, 29
  warm, 58, 72-3
  white and, 118
rustic look, 64

S

Scandinavian style, muted colours, 66
sea colours, 7, 12, 35-40
secondary colours, definition, 10
shade, definition, 10
Shaker style, muted colours, 66
shell pink, 78-9
single-colour schemes, 19
sky colours, 7, 12, 35-40
small rooms, 18
studies, brown, 122
sunny colours, 13
sunrise and sunset colours, 6, 29-34
sunset colours, 6

T

terracotta, 81-86
  ethnic look, 84-5
  other colours with, 86
  pale shades, 82-3
  rich, 84-5
  spicy touches, 82-3
textiles, textured, 54-5
textures
  floors, 54
  textiles, 54-5
  wall, 52-3
ticking, 55
tint, definition, 10
tone, definition, 10
turquoise, 103-9
  blue shades, 104-5
  green shades, 106-7

W

wall textures, neutral colours and, 52-3
wallpapers, co-ordinating, 20
warm colours, 5, 6
  cool rooms, 34
  definition, 10
  effect of, 31
  Provençal, 23
white, 115-20
  as an accent, 119
  black and, 120
  blue and, 118
  earth colours and, 47
  green and, 118
  light and, 116
  neutral colours and, 56

pale combinations, 116-17
red and, 118
yellow and, 118
wool flannel, 55
working areas, 18, 122

Y

yellows, 91-6
  blues and, 96
  cool, 94-5
  effect of light on, 95
  hot, 92-3
  pastels, 41-4
  shades of, 92
  sunrise and sunset colours, 29, 33
  white and, 118

ACKNOWLEDGEMENTS

Photographs: 5 Elizabeth Whiting and Associates/Spike Powell, 6-8(t) Eaglemoss/Tif Hunter, 8(b) Ideal-Standard, 8-9(bl),9(t) EM/Tif Hunter, 10 Richard Paul, 11 Robert Harding Syndication/IPC Magazines, 12(bl,cr) Eaglemoss/Graham Rae, (br) Robert Harding Syndication/IPC Magazines, 12-13(t) Robert Harding Syndication/IPC Magazines, 13(bl) Eaglemoss/Graham Rae, (br) Robert Harding Syndication/IPC Magazines, 14(t,bl) Eaglemoss/Graham Rae, (bl) The Merchant Tiler, 15(cr) Eaglemoss/Graham Rae, (br) Robert Harding Syndication/IPC Magazines, 16(t) Arthur Sanderson and Sons, (b) Elizabeth Whiting and Associates/Nick Carter, 17 Eaglemoss/Steve Tanner, 19 Dulux, 20(l) Eaglemoss/Steve Tanner, 20-21 Liberty, 22(t) Ken Kirkwood, (bl) Ronseal, (br) Eaglemoss/Steve Tanner, 23 Eaglemoss/Tif Hunter, 24(t) Maison de Marie Claire/Nicolas/Postic, (c) Insight, London/Michelle Garrett, (b) Houses and Interiors, 25(t) Houses and Interiors, (b) Ken Kirkwood, 26(tl) Ken Kirkwood, (bl) Bill McLaughlin, 26-7(t) Insight, London/Michelle Garrett, (cr) Elizabeth Whiting and Associates/Tom Leighton, (br) Eaglemoss/Steve Tanner, 28(t) Bill McLaughlin, (b) Maison de Marie Claire/Giraudon/Peuch, 29 Eaglemoss/Steve Tanner, 30(t) Crown Paints, 30-1 Arthur Sanderson and Sons, 32 Dulux, 33(t) Dulux, (b) Crown Paints, 34(t) Elizabeth Whiting and Associates/Di Lewis, (b) Arthur Sanderson and Sons, 35 Eaglemoss/Tif Hunter, 36(t) Crown Paints, (bl) Swish, (br) Elizabeth Whiting and Associates/Rodney Hyett, 37(t) Robert Harding Picture Library, (b) Arcaid/Julie Phipps, 38(t) Elizabeth Whiting and Associates/Di Lewis, (b) Crown Paints, 39(t) Crown Paints, (b) Elizabeth Whiting and Associates/Spike Powell, 40(t) Modes et Travaux, (b) Crown Paints, 41 Eaglemoss/Tif Hunter, 42(bl) Richard Paul, 42-43 Elizabeth Whiting and Associates, 43(tr) Bo Appeltoft, (br) Elizabeth Whiting and Associates/Spike Powell, 44(t) Ken Kirkwood, (br) Eaglemoss/Mal Stone, 45 Eaglemoss/Tif Hunter, 46-7 Richard Paul, 48(tl) Richard Paul, (tr) Elizabeth Whiting and Associates/Neil Lorimer, (b) Elizabeth Whiting and Associates/June Buck, 49(t) Mondadori Press/Buralti/Xerra, (bl) Whiteheads Fabrics, (b) Cristal Tiles, 50(t) René Stoeltie, (bl) Elizabeth Bradley Designs, (br) René Stoeltie, 51 Ideal-Standard, 52(t) Cent Idées/Dirand/Lebeau, (b) Houses and Interiors, 53(tl) Dulux, (bl) Deidi von Schaewen, (br) Kingfisher, 54(t) Houses and Interiors, (b) Ken Kirkwood, 55(t) Maison de Marie Claire/Nicolas/Postic, (b) Crown Paints, 56(t) Crowson Fabrics, (bl)

Elizabeth Whiting and Associates/Michael Dunne, (br) Ametex, 57 Eaglemoss/Tif Hunter, 58(t) Marks and Spencer, (b) Houses and Interiors, 59(t) Eaglemoss/Steve Tanner, (b) Arthur Sanderson and Sons, 60 Elizabeth Whiting and Associates/Michael Dunne, 61(t) Ken Kirkwood, (b) Elizabeth Whiting and Associates/Jon Bouchier, 62(t) Arthur Sanderson and Sons, (bl) Forbo-Mayfair, (br) Elizabeth Whiting and Associates/Andreas von Einsiedel, 63 Eaglemoss/Tif Hunter, 64 Arthur Sanderson and Sons, 65(tr) Elizabeth Whiting and Associates, (bl) Eaglemoss/John Suett, (br) Ken Kirkwood, 66(t) Marks and Spencer, (b) Mondadori Press/Nocentini/Frateschi, 67(tl) Ken Kirkwood, (b) Crown Paints, 68(t) Fired Earth, (b) René Stoeltie, 69 Eaglemoss/Graham Rae, 70(t) Insight, London/Michelle Garrett, (b) Elizabeth Whiting and Associates/Andreas von Einsiedel, 71(t) Elizabeth Whiting and Associates/Neil Lorimer, (bl) Eaglemoss/Graham Rae, (br) Ariadne, Holland, 72(t) Houses and Interiors, (b) Elizabeth Whiting and Associates/Spike Powell, 73(t) Eaglemoss/Graham Rae, (b) Elizabeth Whiting and Associates/Di Lewis, 74(t) Eaglemoss/Graham Rae, (tr) Ariadne, Holland, (b) Parker Knoll, 75 Eaglemoss/Graham Rae, 76(tl) Eaglemoss/Simon Page-Ritchie, (tr) Elizabeth Whiting and Associates/Spike Powell, (b) Smallbone of Devizes, 77(t) Laura Ashley, (b) Eaglemoss/Simon Page-Ritchie, 78(t) Eaglemoss/Simon Page-Ritchie, (c) Elizabeth Whiting and Associates/Spike Powell, (b) Elizabeth Whiting and Associates/Michael Nicholson, 79 Elizabeth Whiting and Associates/Spike Powell, 80(t) Richard Paul, (b) Elizabeth Whiting and Associates/Andreas von Einsiedel, 81 Designers' Guild, 82(tl) Eaglemoss/Graham Rae, (tr) Ingrid Mason Picture Library/Marie-Louise Avery, (b) Elizabeth Whiting and Associates/Spike Powell, 83(t) Bo Appeltoft, (c) Insight, London, (b) Eaglemoss/Graham Rae, 84(t) Osborne and Little by Nina Campbell, (bl) Eaglemoss/Graham Rae, (br) Marie Claire Maison/Hallard/Bailhache, 85(t,br) Eaglemoss/Graham Rae, (c) Houses and Interiors, (bl) Elizabeth Whiting and Associates/June Buck, 86(tl) Eaglemoss/Graham Rae, (cr) Conran Octopus/Ianthe Ruthven, (b) Ariadne, Holland, 87 Eaglemoss/Graham Rae, 88(tl) Eaglemoss/Graham Rae, (tr) Insight, London, (bl) Eaglemoss/Graham Rae, (br) Houses and Interiors, 89(t) Smallbone of Devizes, (bl) Eaglemoss/Steve Tanner, (b) Eaglemoss/Graham Rae, (b) Mondadori Press, 91 Crown Paints, 92(t) Bo Appeltoft, (b) René Stoeltie, 92-93(b) Richard Paul, 93(t) Bo Appeltoft, (br) Elizabeth Whiting and Associates/Andreas von Einsiedel, 94(t) Elizabeth Whiting and Associates/Peter Woloszynski, (b) Elizabeth Whiting and Associates/Spike Powell,

95(tl) S&O Mathews, (tr) Ken Kirkwood, (b) Insight, London/Linda Burgess, 96(tl) Jane Churchill, (tr) Houses and Interiors, (b) Designers' Guild, 97 Eaglemoss/Graham Rae, 98(t) Designers' Guild, (bl) Eaglemoss/Steve Tanner, (br) Boys Syndication, 99(t) Eaglemoss/Steve Tanner, (b) Designers' Guild, 100(tl) Elizabeth Whiting and Associates/Rodney Hyett, (tr) Romo Fabrics, (b) Eaglemoss/Steve Tanner, 101 Osborne and Little by Nina Campbell, 102(t) Ariadne, Holland, (b) Aquaware, 103 Eaglemoss/Graham Rae, 104(t) Eaglemoss/Graham Rae, (b) Robert Harding Syndication/IPC/Homes and Gardens, (b) Maison de Marie Claire/Hussenot/Puech, 106(bl) Robert Harding Syndication/IPC Magazines, 106-7(bc) Crown Paints, 107(t) Eaglemoss/Graham Rae, (b) Habitat, 108(t) Elizabeth Whiting and Associates, (b) Sue Atkinson/Arc Studios, 109 Eaglemoss/Graham Rae, 110(t) Sue Atkinson/Arc Studios, (b) Elizabeth Whiting and Associates/Rodney Hyett, 110-111(tc) Maison de Marie Claire/Hussenot/Puech, 111(tr) Eaglemoss/Graham Rae, (bl) Elizabeth Whiting and Associates/David George/Cassell, (br) Deschamps, 112(t) Elizabeth Whiting and Associates/Gary Chowanetz, (b) Ingrid Mason Picture Library/Marie-Louise Avery, 113(t,bl) Eaglemoss/Graham Rae, (c) Boys Syndication, (br) G-Plan, 114(t) Elizabeth Whiting and Associates/Michael Dunne, (c) Arcaid/Julie Phipps, (b) Eaglemoss/Graham Rae, 115 Eaglemoss/Simon Page-Ritchie, 116(t) Laura Ashley, (c) Maison de Marie Claire/Hirsch, (b) Elizabeth Whiting and Associates/Spike Powell, 117(t) Eaglemoss/Simon Page-Ritchie, (b) Ken Kirkwood, 118(tl) Eaglemoss/Simon Page-Ritchie, (tr) Arcaid/Richard Bryant, (b) Richard Paul, 119(tl) Eaglemoss/Simon Page-Ritchie, (b) Robert Harding Picture Library, (c) Eaglemoss/Simon Page-Ritchie, (br) Ingrid Mason Picture Library, 120(t) Ariadne, Holland, (cr) Elizabeth Whiting and Associates/Judith Patrick, (b) Elizabeth Whiting and Associates/Rodney Hyett, 121 Eaglemoss/Graham Rae, 122(t) Robert Harding Syndication/IPC Magazines, (bl) Arcaid/Ken Kirkwood, (br) Eaglemoss/Graham Rae, 123(tl) Eaglemoss/Graham Rae, (tr) Robert Harding Syndication/IPC/Homes and Gardens, (b) Robert Harding Syndication/IPC Magazines, 124(t) Laura Ashley, (b) Eaglemoss/Adrian Taylor, 125(tl) Robert Harding Syndication/IPC/Country Homes and Interiors, (tr) Eaglemoss/Adrian Taylor, (b) Crown Berger, 126(t) Arthur Sanderson and Sons, (bl) Eaglemoss/Graham Rae, (br) Laura Ashley.